Ben Baker's

Festive

Double Issue

Forty Years of Christmas TV

For Roland.

Introduction

Christmas. What does it mean to you?

Don't answer that out loud, obviously. This is a book, not Google. If you're British, the festive season invariably means excess – be it through food, drink or most importantly for this book – television, which gets more and more interesting and away from the regular schedule the closer we get to the big day. Indeed, it never fails to baffle me that most American TV programmes run their big festive specials around December 9th then just show repeats for a month when we in good old Blighty Britain are nowhere near ready to see so much as a televised paper hat until the very week of Jesus's birth.

To us, Christmas television is a serious business and as essential to the experience as crackers, sprouts and avoiding a hairy-lipped snog from your Great Auntie Carol whose breath smells like Sugar Puffs. Whether it's Morecambe and Wise recreating "Singin' In The Rain", Del and Rodney dressed as the Dynamic Duo or the ever-miserable characters of "EastEnders" running over a baby for some light relief, TV is our very pal throughout the entire turkey and tinsel period. Even the adverts are held in just as much high fascination with many of my friends getting far too excited for that 30-year old footage of the *"holidays are coming"* Coca Cola truck appear on the horizon and imagining which song you previously liked John Lewis ruin this year with a dreary, half-speed cover version.

To make sure we take in as much as possible of the telly available in late December, the purchasing of a Christmas TV Guide is still an essential ritual for many households, even when the programme information is easily accessed on every digital device you can cram into your fist. Seeing the festive, double-length bumper edition of the Radio Times (and its cheaper, if less exciting ilk) for the first time remains genuinely exciting - even if it's immediately followed by an exclamation of "HOW BLOODY MUCH?" And even when we know it can't possibly live up to thrills of Christmas telly in the past and you saw all the films years ago, there's still a huge pleasure in going through the whole issue with a big pen to ring the "can't miss" shows.

My aim with this book is to recreate the giddy fun of those TV periodicals of yesteryear with a day-by-day look at the full festive fortnight, from the first flush of school's out excitement to those desperate moments wringing out the last drops of cheer on entering the New Year. I'll be taking my big red pen to the best and worst tinsel-topped telly from years past, along with the weird, the wonderful and the "still facing charges pending further inquiry".

To help preserve this yellowing nostalgic window into the past I've kept the period covered in the book between 1955 and 1995 which I feel reflects the boom and bust of the traditional family experience of watching television before every home had multiple TV sets, hundreds of barely-watchable digital channels and nobody could drift off playing Candy Crush on their smart phones. And I bloody love playing Candy Crush on my smart phone whilst ignoring my parents, but there's something special about the communal viewing environment which provided so many laughs, tears and tantrums because the family voted to watch "Annie" rather than the "Supergran" Christmas special on the other side.

I plan for this book to touch on the "classics" of Decembers past that everyone talks about alongside the other shows in the schedule that slipped down the back of time's sofa long ago Who needs two pages of me asking if you remember that time Dirty Den said "Ooh, I am right divorcing you, Ange!" when I could be talking about Kid Creole's strange post-watershed musical about racism, Roland Rat going to Switzerland or Feargal Sharkey having a nightmare on a Concorde whilst the Krankies watch on in helpless bemusement high above the Telecom Tower? All of those are in this book, along with over 250 other entries from back in the day.

To keep things simpler and not have to explain to the under thirties about things such as in-vision continuity and localised birthday rabbits, I've simplified every credit for the third channel to just "ITV" rather than the regional broadcaster it may have originally aired on. Likewise for BBC programmes before it split into two channels I've gone with the simple credit of "BBC".

Grab a sherry and pull up a chair because as Noddy Holder from Slade informs us every December time in his loudest voice, "THE GRIIIIIMMMMMLLLLLEEEEYYYYSSSS IS ONNNNNN!" Also: Christmas.

Merry Everybody!

Your very pal,

Ben Baker

December 22nd

There's always going to be debate about when the Christmas period truly starts. In America, it seems to be from the very second the last Thanksgiving Day float leaves Times Square, whilst in the UK, many still use the age old tradition of "Builder's Friday" - the last day on site for manual workers - who honour the occasion by knocking off early to drink fourteen pints and vomit copiously in the taxi home.

When it comes to television, we could mark the start of the season with regular daytime programming being swapped out by the moth-eaten appearance of "St Trinians And The Carry On Up The Yellowing Film Of That Darn Digby The Biggest Railway Dinosaur In The World: The Movie" in the schedules with barely a Shrek to go round. Since 2004, we've also had the diminishing returns of the new "The X Factor" winner being announced, although the show's assault on the Christmas pop charts seems to have thankfully waned with many of its winners surviving only slightly longer than the average mayfly. For me, you really know its coming up to the festive period when someone on "EastEnders" suddenly declares "I love Christmas, me and am definitely going to live forever up to and including Christmas Day!"?

Because we have to start somewhere, for the purposes of this book I've selected December 22nd as when the Christmas period truly begins. By now all the schools should have broken up for the holidays and workplaces shouldn't be far behind. At home, the tree is up while snowflake and robin-tinged cards should adorn a number of previously boring flat surfaces and impromptu lengths of string. And somewhere in the living room, the Grattan or Argos catalogue is still "accidentally" lying around after you spent most of the previous five weeks hopefully circling its gifty goodies and only occasionally sneaking a peek at the bra section. Oh well. Shall we begin..?

Thursday 22nd December, 1955

9.00pm: The Man Who Liked Christmas (ITV)

Just liked it, mind. Don't get carried away. This was the 13th episode of ITV's long-running "London Playhouse" presentations courtesy of weekday licence holder Associated Rediffusion. The network had launched in a sea of promotional toothpaste only four months earlier on the 22nd September 1955 but at this point was only being seen in the capital[1]. The script for "The Man Who Liked Christmas" was by the Canadian playwright Reuben Ship who originally wrote it in 1953 for CBC Radio in his home country. The following year he had become mildly infamous after turning his experience with the Communist witch-finder hearings into a radio satire called "The Investigator" in which a McCarthy-esque senator tries to talk his way into Heaven. Whilst never officially broadcast in the US, it was bootlegged heavily and the reaction probably inspired Ship's move to England shortly after to pursue a career in advertising.

A huge coup for this play was the casting of David Kossoff in the lead role after his recent 1954 BAFTA award for Most Promising Newcomer to Film. British audiences of a certain age would probably know him best however from the ITV sitcom "The Larkins"(1958-64). He was also the father of Paul Kossoff, guitarist in British rockers Free. Upon Paul's death in 1976, aged just 25 from a pulmonary embolism, his father became a vehement anti-drug campaigner and established The Paul Kossoff Foundation to explain the realities of drug addiction to children. What a jolly start to the book…

---

1   ITV would eventually expanded the following year, starting with the Midlands in February 1956 then the rest of the North.

Saturday 22nd December, 1962

5.00pm: The Boss Cat (BBC)

"A new film cartoon series about the gang of alley cats."

The renaming of Hanna-Barbera's most intellectual (yet living in a bin) *Top Cat* due to a name clash with a British cat food product available at the time is now fairly well known among animation fans and bin-based cat cartoon conspiracy theorists. In fact the series <u>had</u> actually launched under its original U.S. title on the BBC in May 1962[2] only being renamed after four episodes had aired due to the legal trouble. These changes did not extend to subbing the series however and close friends still got to call him TC. From December 1962 the dignified pantsless feline would become a staple of Saturday nights for the next four months alongside British favourites "Dixon of Dock Green", "Juke Box Jury" and this...

5.25pm: Mr Pastry's Pet Shop (BBC)

Richard Hearne's Cairoli-lite character Mr Pastry was a staple on post-war TV – even making guest appearances on Ed Sullivan's huge variety series in America - but the titular pet shop owner would be forever known in our house as "that miserable old c**t" after the walrus-tashed favourite had refused to give my dad an autograph as a kid. Both Hearne and Pastry seem now largely forgotten by modern audiences, due to most of his output being wiped. Maybe he should have been nicer to me dad, eh?

---

2   A month after the single 30-episode season concluded in the US.

Wednesday 22nd December, 1965

5.50pm: The Magic Roundabout (BBC One)

"A film series from France. Episode 39: Roundabout Christmas.[3] *"*

How much does that simple five-word introduction undersell the joy, humour and personality of Eric Thompson's wonderful reworking of Serge Danot's French animation "Le Manège Enchanté"[4]? Sadly awkward rights hell means, other than the odd but wonderful spin-off film "Dougal and The Blue Cat", "The Magic Roundabout" has yet to grace DVD and probably never will, which is a crying shame as some episodes only seemingly ever aired once and deserve to be rediscovered by another generation who probably only know the characters from novelty retro pencil cases and (hopefully not) that dire 2005 CGI film[5]. Even Nigel Planer's fun revival co-written with his brother Roger for Channel Four in the early 1990s seems to have all but vanished from the face of the planet. A shame for kids of all ages.

---

[3] A Christmas themed story based on Thompson's script featured in the book "The Adventures Of Dylan" (Bloomsbury, 1998)

[4] Although the animation was mostly done by the Paris-based English animator Ivor Wood (1932–2004) who would go on to animate most of the next several generation's childhoods from Paddington, The Herbs and The Wombles to his own Woodland Animations productions Postman Pat, Charlie Chalk and Bertha. Also Gran but that was rubbish.

[5] The two disc version DVD of which did feature some black and white "Magic Roundabout" episodes as extras but I'm still sulking anyway.

Friday 22nd December, 1967

12.10am: God with a Face (ITV)

"A conversation about Christmas between The Bishop of Woolwich and Howard Williams of Bloomsbury Central Baptist Church."

If God had a face, what would it be? I'm thinking it'd be a sort of spoon faced dragon. With six breasts. This was the last in a series of five bedtime theological leg-rubbers over Christmas 1967 and it's no surprise that all the kids were asking for their very own "Bishop of Woolwich Fun Book" and Stretch Howard Williams dolls under the tree that year. (This is a lie.)

Saturday 22nd December, 1968

3.55pm: Bugs Bunny Nips the Nips (ITV)

"A Merrie Melodies Cartoon In Technicolour"

Originally produced in April 1944, here's a jolly romp for all the kiddies at Christmas in which the carrot-crunching comic character lays waste to a myriad of Japanese stereotypes supposedly to help America's brave boys fighting the foreign types during World War 2. Despite its unrepentantly stereotypical view of the US's then-enemy, this Friz Freleng-produced short wasn't included in Warner Bros' infamous "Censored Eleven", a series of 11 shorts from the 1930s and 1940s that had been pulled from syndication, due to changing times and discomfort over ignorant (if not malicious) racial content but understandably hasn't been seen very much since.

Tuesday 22nd December, 1970

10.10pm: Monty Python's Flying Circus (BBC One)

The second and probably best run of "Flying Circus" comes to an end with "Royal Episode 13" one of its most controversial episodes. Opening with a joke that at any point The Queen might be tuning in (although is invariably watching "The Virginian"[6]), outraging many admittedly easily-outraged sorts in 1970 when Her Maj was generally considered off the market for gags. Another running theme about cannibalism is even more off-colour climaxing as it does with the infamous "Undertaker" sketch with Graham Chapman suggesting that a customer should eat his recently deceased mother. In protest, members of the studio audience are seen to storm the stage in an alarmingly realistic fashion, only stopped from rioting by the National Anthem which signifies that the Queen has finally switched the show on. With the reaction the original footage had received by the public[7] this final sketch was ear-marked for removal from future repeats. As such, when it came to releasing the episodes on VHS, the original recording had seemingly disappeared and a lower quality 525-line NTSC broadcast copy from US television had to be spliced in giving an eerie out-of-reality glow to the already unsettling scene.

---

6   A strange choice because U.S. western serial "The Virginian" was a BBC One programme – the same channel this instalment of *Flying Circus* was first shown on. The most recent episode then being shown on Friday 18th December 1970 at 6:45pm.

7   Rev. Francis Coveney writing to the Radio Times to *"seriously suggest that people who can think up this sort of rubbish should consult a psychoanalyst before they proceed any further."* His reaction to the line *"You wouldn't know the difference between the Battle of Borodino and a tiger's bum"* - also in this episode – remains sadly unrecorded.

Saturday 22nd December, 1973

3.10pm: International Sports Special – Christmas Darts Spectacular (ITV)

"Eight show-business stars pair off with eight darts "professionals" - in the first ever Pro-Am type competition."

A "World of Sport" special with *"at least £1,000 in prize money"* featuring the cream of 1973's availability; DJ Ed Stewart, pop's Engelbert Humperdinck, heavyweight Joe Bugner, then-Brighton and Hove manager Brian Clough, actress and singer Anita Harris, TV Doctor Robin Nedwell, Fred Trueman off of "Indoor League" and eventual victor, the bowler-bonced jazz man Acker Bilk. Those who know their Light Entertainment will find it no surprise that the Variety Club of Great Britain were involved and among the prizes were *"special TV Times Christmas turkeys that the show-business players can win for charity every time they score more than 80!"* Phwoar!

Sunday, 22nd December, 1974

1.30pm: Star Trek – The Animated Series (BBC One)

Produced by infamous cheapo cartoon house Filmation, the animated "Star Trek" was surprisingly a cut above their usual fare thanks in part to the appearance of the full live action series' crew plus writers from the original show contributing scripts. Here in the UK this animated version of everyone's favourite 'starsmen' had been a hit on Saturday teatimes throughout 1974 and repeats of the original show ran all that Christmas under the awkward title "Holiday Star Trek". It's a shame you don't get repeat showings renamed with lame attempts to tie into the season anymore; who wouldn't love to see the likes of "Holiday Still Open All Hours", "Holiday The Martin Lewis Money Show" and "Holiday Holiday '96" in the schedule?

Sunday, 22nd December, 1974

3.50pm: Basil Brush's Christmas Fantasy (BBC One)

Losing a little of his earlier pull thanks to the likes of that new-fangled Emu, Basil was nonetheless a Christmas regular with new specials right up to 1980, including "Basil's Christmas in Norway" (1975), "Basil Through the Looking Glass" (1977), "Basil in Neverland" (1976) and "Basil's Christmas in the Country" (1979) all of which sound positively... on once. Back in 1974, Basil would pop up again on the 25th as part of BBC One's then-traditional visitin' the sick kiddies slot "A Stocking Full Of Stars" with Michael Aspel, Showaddywaddy, Michael Crawford and um…Rolf Harris direct from the National Children's Home at Harpenden. I hope the kids asked for vodka and a pistol that Christmas...

Monday, 22nd December, 1975

8.00pm: Lawrence of Arabia – Part One (ITV)

"Lt. Lawrence, an idealistic young officer, wins an assignment to the camp of Prince Feisal, leader of the Arab revolt against the Turks..."

For someone born in the eighties like myself, big Hollywood

blockbuster films like "Gone with the Wind", "Ben Hur" and this 1962 epic seemed fairly commonplace each holiday period on TV and therefore appeared to be lengthy old dullness I didn't need to trouble myself with, unless I wanted to get a few more references on "Muppet Babies". Only when old enough to appreciate these benchmarks of American film did I learn that they were surprisingly quite fresh to TV; the studios had regularly returned them to hugely profitable repeat runs in cinemas, in those simpler times before home recordings. There was a sea change approaching, and between 1974 and 1977, many blockbusting epics that were once the backbone of the local fleapit made it to telly. The concept was so new that only two months before "Lawrence" aired, on 28th October 1975, "Dr. No" had become the first Bond film to appear on telly.

With its structure already handily broken into two parts in the original full film, it made perfect sense for ITV to split David Lean's groaning three-and-a-half-hour feature over two consecutive nights. The TV Times was so excited they even added a cartoon of Peter O'Toole to its Christmas front cover, where he shared space with Les Dawson, Barbara Windsor's Bosoms and Sooty. Despite all this fanfare, the film did not rate highly; part one going up against a BBC One line up of "Born Free" (also receiving its own British television première), plus "Are You Being Served?" and the "Mastermind" final.

Saturday 22nd December, 1979

10.30am: TISWAS (ITV)

"If you want culture, education, serious discussion and politics – you won't find them here"

Itching to get going after a ten-week industrial dispute took ITV off the air, the Saturday morning kids hotchpotch "TISWAS" began its sixth series in November 1979 and, unlike its early regional days, was now shown in most of the UK, becoming a home for the disparate likes of Frank Carson, Lenny Henry and Bob Carolgees. This was the era of "The Bucket of Water Song" getting in the Top 40, Sally James interviewing The Clash and comedy guests like Terry Jones turning up to promote "Life of Brian" - a film none of the target audience could actually go and see - simply because it seemed like a laugh. This 1979 Christmas show featured the obligatory "Scrooge" parody with former Scaffold member John Gorman as the miserable old sod while Bob, Sally, Norman Collier and, of course, Spit The Dog play to the crowd as the poor "Family Scratchspit". There was also a live cow in the studio. Elsewhere "Christmas Compost Corner" had Carson in full terrible gag flow and there was music from the comedy pop act The Barron Knights who were back in the charts after a welcome break and whom we'll sadly hear more of later in the book. The peak of in both popularity and quality would come in 1980-81 so few were surprised at the end of it when the whole cast – minus Sally – announced they were off to conquer late night adult TV. My god I wish they hadn't.

6:35pm: Christmas Snowtime Special (BBC One)

"Recorded in the village of Leysin, Switzerland. Introduced by Dame Edna Everage (a member of the Barry Humphries group)."

Quite what the official sounding "Barry Humphries group" entails is a question for a higher power than I, but you can't knock the collective star quality in this slice of cheery Eurofluff; Abba, Leo Sayer, The Jacksons, Boney M and Bonnie Tyler. Never mind that most of it had been culled from various other BBC "spectaculars" filmed around the same time for budget saving reasons. The highlight for non-pop Swede obsessives would probably have to be Kate Bush singing the slight but delightful festive tune "December Will Be Magic Again" for the first time on TV, a whole year before it was released as a single in November 1980. If you were bereft of recording equipment though there was a second chance to hear the new song when it was performed as part of Bush's own TV special "Kate" broadcast six days later on BBC Two.

11.15pm: The Secret Policeman's Ball (ITV)

"A record of the Amnesty International charity show at Her Majesty's Theatre in the Haymarket, London, in June."

To be in attendance for one of these late-night Amnesty shows in the late seventies must have been something like a Comedy 101 course for anyone asleep for the previous two decades. A rare chance to see people like Alan Bennett, Eleanor Bron and the Pythons who had long since become household names and even National Treasure status doing the sort of acts they originally made their names with. Whilst the first two revues – 1976's "A Poke in the Eye (With a Sharp Stick)" and 1977's "The Mermaid Frolics" – produced by John Cleese and Terry Jones respectively – were fun greatest hits sets by many of the previous generation of comics, "The Secret Policeman's Ball" was the first to feel more in tune with the new wave of comedy coming through, in part due to the inclusion of the extremely rude Billy Connolly, along with a 24-year-old Rowan Atkinson. The highlight for many was a fired-up Peter Cook's parody of the extremely topical[8] summation of Judge Joseph Cantley's appallingly biased attack on several witnesses during his summation of the Jeremy Thorpe case[9]. Cook's solo turn was so popular it was released as a single by Virgin Records under the title "Here Comes the Judge – Live" and forever giving the world the immortal phrase *"a self-confessed player of the pink oboe"*. Amazingly, Cook only came up with the routine for the third night of the show (Friday, 29th June, 1979) when a scabrous *Daily Telegraph* review of its first evening had chided the lack of new material.

A longer theatrical film of the show, featuring more comedy items and musical performances from Pete Townshend and Tom Robinson would appear in cinemas the following June. A follow-up show entitled "The Secret Policeman's Other Ball" would eventually take place in September 1981 by which time the political landscape was very different.

Thursday 22nd December, 1983

9.00am: Roland's Winter Wonderland (ITV)

"The three rodents decorate their superstar alpine chalet."

Everyone knows how Roland Rat effectively saved TV-am (*"rat joins sinking ship ha ha"*, copyright Every Rotten Newspaper Ever) with his Spectacular Shedvision Show segments but, with the full support of new Editor-in-Chief Greg Dyke, the cool

---

8 The shows were performed at the end of June 1979 – less than two weeks after the trial's collapse.

9 As recently dramatized in BBC One's "A Very English Scandal"

puppet genuinely was a saviour for the struggling service connecting with audiences young and old. It's not hard to see why; David Claridge's puppet was modern, could interact wittily with humans around him and was as obsessed with celebrity as many of his young fans who rushed out to buy his dolls, games, books and even the truly awful "Rat Rapping" single. All this attracted even more viewers to his early morning segments which had progressed from the Shed to outside broadcasts for *Rat On The Road* in the summer holidays and for Christmas, a trip to Switzerland on a limited budget for some pre-recorded links by Roland, Kevin the Gerbil and put-upon Welsh miserablist Errol the Hamster. Over two million viewers tuned in. The next holiday period, Easter 1984, saw them travel even further afield, to Hong Kong; for "Roland Goes East", now joined by his hyperactive stowaway brother Little Reggie.

The following year, Roland would famously burrow out of breakfast TV and into the Beeb in a controversial transfer. "Roland's Yuletide Binge" (Christmas Day 1985, 11:30am, BBC One) would announce his glittering arrival at his new home with a fun wander around the studios bumping into various stars of the time including Russell Grant, Ian McCaskill, Frankie Howerd, Beryl Reid and Jan 'Lemming' in the news room. Thanks in part to a script co-written by Richard Curtis, it's a funny and just about stretches to its 25 minute length but lacks the spontaneity and surprise of his earlier breakfast outings with unsuspecting celebrities who were less in on the joke. By the time "Roland Rat – The Series" appeared in September 1986[10] the joke had already worn thin and come the following Christmas Day's special had moved back to the slightly earlier time of 8.45am. As Roland himself might say "NYEHHHH"...

---

[10]   As the only lead-in *Doctor Who: Trial of a Time Lord* truly deserved.

Saturday 22nd December, 1984

6.50pm: Russ Abbot's Christmas Madhouse (ITV)

8.50pm: Tarby and Christmas Friends (ITV)

A double bill of low-level laughs from Les Dennis and Dustin Gee, who were in high demand appearing on both ITV programmes that December evening, despite already moving to the BBC for their own series[11]. Things were even more frantic in Christmas 1985 as the pair were in pantomime in Merseyside and launched the third run of "Les and Dustin's Laughter Show". Sadly, Gee wouldn't get to see the second episode go out due to his sudden and shocking death on January 3rd 1986 from heart problems, aged just 43. Even worse, the panto had to continue and so it was that Jim Bowen agreed to step in to fill the role two days after Gee's death with a crushed Dennis still obliged to finish the production he began barely a fortnight earlier with his old friend and mentor.

10.00pm: There's Something Wrong in Paradise (ITV)

"A magical musical set on the mythical Caribbean island of Zyllha. Kid Creole and his Coconuts are shipwrecked on the island, ruled by President Nignat, who believes in racial purity. He is incensed by the Kid's mixed-race group winning his island's music festival."

How amazing does this sound? A two-hour musical set around the music of Kid Creole And The Coconuts, one of the biggest

---

[11] That same year, the duo had bravely battled on through their act whilst a dying Tommy Cooper lay just off-stage during the April 15th edition of "Live From Her Majesty's".

chart acts of recent years tackling racial hatred with songs from their back catalogue including the title song from the band's underperforming new album Doppelgänger. Unfortunately, even with the terrific Pauline Black from The Selecter as Mimi, The Three Degrees and Oscar-nominee Karen Black, the whole thing is a bit tedious, framed like an old Hollywood musical but confined to the studio and produced on ugly looking videotape. Creole himself - or August Darnell to his mam – is fine as a leading man but the surprisingly serious script by Mustapha Matura with its central theme of racial unrest and guerrilla uprising doesn't quite gel with the upbeat funky 80s pop of the Coconuts. This tough subject might explain the surprisingly late 10pm timeslot which will have excluded any younger fans. With Granada producing the special, it's not too surprising that Kid Creole was kicking around on set when "12-year-old Chorister of the Year" David Pickering turned up for their Christmas Eve special "Joy to the World". Described in that year's TV Times as a *"magical tour of Christmas past and present"*, the special found Pickering touring round the broadcaster's then-new Studio One complex whilst meeting any available stars. And we still never learned who Annie's daddy was…

Monday, 22nd December, 1986

10.20am: The Toughest Man in the World (ITV)

"Vietnam veteran Bruise Brubaker runs a youth centre for troubled youngsters. When he learns that the centre will have to close, Bruise agrees to enter a contest with a first prize of $100,000."

The huge success in the 1980s of the gold chain-laden Mr T must seem an oddity to people not living thorough those times yet when the comedy drama one-off TV movie "The Toughest Man in the World" first appeared in November 1984, this professional fool pitier was arguably the most recognisable person on planet Earth. Originally aired on CBS in America at the same time as the third series of "The A Team", the film is not notable for much, although second billed actor Dennis Dugan swapped performing for directing and has since made pretty much every Adam Sandler vehicle since 1996 including "I Now Pronounce You Chuck and Larry", "Grown Ups", "Jack and Jill" and countless other "fun" adventures about permanent man-children and the awful nagging attractive women they married. Sadly Dugan has yet to find a space for Mr T to appear in any of these cinematic classics. So much pity, so many fools!

12.20pm: A Song for Christmas (BBC One)

"Phillip Schofield presents the first of three programmes to find this year's Song for Christmas."

1986's Pebble Mill spin-off "A Song For Christmas" was a short-lived yearly nationwide contest for schools across the country to write and perform an entirely original festive composition on TV in front of a panel containing pop mega-stars. In 1986, this included Bucks Fizz new girl Shelley Preston, songwriter and Mike Batt plus chairman Peter Skellern. The winning song in question was "A Child of Peace" from a school in Rhydyfelin[12], Wales, beating into second place the sax-drenched power ballad "Let's Pray for Christmas" sung by a self-confident 15- year-old from Cheshire called Gary Barlow, four years away from being the one nobody liked much in Take

---

12   Which I believe is one of the ingredients in Ribena.

That. The clip of Barlow would later appear on a lot of shows after he hit stardom but for all his admittedly comical snood-wearing earnest pretentiousness, the song shows his genuine song-writing talent at a strikingly early age. The whole story was recounted for a brilliant Radio Wales documentary in 2014 suitably titled "Take That Gary Barlow!", which is very worth tracking down. As for Gary, the "Love Wont Wait" multi-millionaire is currently somewhere spending his money. Hope this helps!

Thursday, 22nd December, 1988

5.05pm: Grow Biz Quiz (BBC Two)

"A star-spangled Grow Biz Quiz special comes to the conservatory tonight as Alan Titchmarsh asks the questions. Beryl Reid, Bill Oddie, Rosalind Runcie and Michael Fish show how they handle a spade, a fork and a 'hoe, hoe, hoe', while Trevor Harrison as Eddie Grundy tempts these celebrity contestants with his own particular brand of festive fare."

No, you're alright ta. ...NEXT!

December 23rd

And so here we are. Another day closer to the big one and unless you're one of those unbearable people with self-control, you should have demolished most of your advent calendar by now all the time constantly eyeing up that double size 'Day 24' section every time the hunger pangs happen. You might even have received your very own Christmas hamper like the ones Gloria Hunniford is always trying trick old people into buying even though there's a very real chance they might cark it before New Year.

In town, there's a genuine sense of thrill (or mild panic for us still behind on our present purchasing) with brass bands and carol singers appearing on the high street whilst department stores run eye-wateringly priced Grottos where your child might be in store for a special present from Santa (although more realistically it'll be a promotional "Fantastic 4: Rise of the Silver Surfer" Frisbee that's been in the stockroom since 2008.) For the grownups, your pasty and coffee places of choice are fully into their extended period of chucking anything even vaguely associated with the season into their "limited edition" recipes, from gingerbread to elf tears.

Despite all the stress, people are nicer, families start to come together and, most importantly, there's something worth watching on the box at long last as the older, less good animated fare of the last twenty years is cracked open. It could be "Shrek". Or "Shrek II". Or even "Shrek". Truly, the possibilities are endless, if not Shrekless.

So pull out your third best box of chocolates and let's see what TV magic appeared on the hallowed December 23rds of yore...

7.00pm: The Phil Silvers Show (ITV)

"Las Vegas Was My Mother's Maiden Name - Harry gets special treatment at a Las Vegas hotel when he is mistaken for the celebrity Phil Silvers!"

Not to be confused with the earlier, actually good Army-set sitcom of the same name this was a disastrous follow up series, featuring Silvers as the Bilko-style fast-talking, money-obsessed and conniving Harry Grafton. Whereas Bilko was an army sergeant, Grafton is a plant foreman and Silvers lost a lot of the in-built underdog status his earlier character had as a poor schmuck in the Army just trying to make a few extra dollars to survive. Here he was instead just a bit of a cheat in a well-paid factory job which was seen as a slap in the face to the hard-working American. Ratings dropped so badly that the series was completely retooled in its last third to quickly parachute in a family as an attempt to centre and humanise the character of Grafton. It didn't work and the series was cancelled at the end of its 30-episode run leaving Silvers to try his hand on the big screen again with turns in "A Funny Thing Happened on the Way to the Forum" and "Carry On Follow That Camel" four years later before a stroke slowed his career. This particular episode was quite a novelty, being shown the same month as its US première and featuring a post-modern premise in which Grafton is mistaken for the real Phil Silvers who apparently exists as a separate entity in that world. And if that's the case, where does Bilko come into it? Who knew that there's some hardcore Phil Silvers multiverse fan fiction just waiting to be written...

10.00pm: Timothy Birdsall (BBC)

"William Rushton introduces some of Timothy Birdsall's unique contributions to That Was The Week That Was."

A tribute to the brilliant cartoonist and writer who had made a name for himself in Private Eye, The Spectator and the afore-mentioned TW3, before his horrendously early death from leukaemia in June 1963 aged just 27. This was a compilation of Birdsall's sketches – in both senses of the word – as he wryly talked the viewer through his quickly drawn cartoons and caricatures usually relating to a topical story or theme of that week. His is a name that deserves to be much better known.

Wednesday, 23rd December 1970

7.20pm: Ace of Clubs - The Grand Final (BBC One)

"Michael Aspel introduces artists competing in the Final of the 1970 Stage Awards from the City Varieties Theatre, Leeds."

From the heart of clubland – back when clubs existed purely on yellowing old film featuring a wobbling "exotic dancer" trying to look unfazed on the orange and puce carpeting encrusted with the pie and peas of a thousand incapable mouths – came this series devoted to finding the best act on the circuit. These were the days when clubs really were a huge deal and TV was a better place for acts being truly honed before they made it on screen. From comics to chanteuses pretty much every big telly star had served their time in the working-men's clubs of old. Whilst most of the "turns" featured have long since faded away, one edition of the series featured not only Norman Collier but also The Grumbleweeds and Paul Daniels. Collier would go on to win the series outright and more importantly the Bernard Delfont Special Award beating singer Peter Firmani, ventriloquist John Bouchier and musical trio Les Sans Nom whose jaunty Bacharach-stuck-in-a-lift grooves on their sole Decca LP "Largely Latin" would have been just the ticket for vinyl DJs surfing the easy listening boom in the late 1990s.

Saturday, 23rd December, 1972

11.00pm: Parkinson (BBC One)

"In a programme specially recorded for Christmas week Michael Parkinson talks to Bing Crosby."

Unlike Parky who will seemingly never die, Bing seems to have been dead forever, existing only on scratchy old black and white film or the ends of festive compilation album. In fact, Bing only left the planet in October 1977 – a month before his last big TV special "Bing Crosby's Merrie Olde Christmas" aired in the US with a certain pop Dame.

Sunday, 23rd December, 1973

1.40pm: Farming Diary (ITV)

"So You Think You Know About Farming? A quiz for Young Farmers in the East of England. This annual event has the reputation of being the most difficult in the young farmer's calendar."

Every time the kids complain there's nothing on, I'm often

reminded by the grey Sundays of my youth with Brian Walden interviewing stuffy old men very slowly and endless refresher courses in whatever language was offering the cheapest package holidays at the time. And then there were the farming reports which I'm sure were very helpful if you were in the industry but the equivalent of watching slurry dry when you're in single figures. As such this trivia battle must have been like an entertainment explosion in the otherwise staid world of cows and some more cows. Sadly the contents of this were not recorded and painstakingly converted to YouTube for me to check so I'll have to defer to the TV Times for more information: *"Ten contestants, one from each area Federation, battle with each other for Farming Diary's coveted award the Silver Bull which will be presented by this year's Miss Anglia."* I think my penis just exploded.

Thursday, 23rd December, 1976

5.40pm: When Santa Rode the Prairie (BBC Two)

"A Festive Western by William Rushton. New Mexico, Christmas Eve 1876 and not a snowflake in sight. Tilly and Charlie Flagstaff have to spend Christmas at the Last Chance Hotel

The joy of doing a book like this is finding out about truly unusual sounding little one-off programmes like this nestling cheerily in the pre-Christmas teatime telly schedules featuring people I really like. Rushton himself plays Santa in this 50 minute fantasy tale featuring songs by him and Roy Civil with a supporting cast that includes future Tomorrow Person Nigel Rhodes, Sue Nicholls and Victor Spinetti. Roy Civil is now a music teacher in the Northampton region.

11.45am: Lyn's Look-In (ITV)

"There's a party in the studio with lots of famous faces from the pop world dropping in to join the fun. And the winner of the Super Christmas Quiz will be announced. So don't forget to look in!"

A staple of North East telly, Lyn Spencer was a Tyne Tees favourite with continuity duties and this was a bit of cheap and cheerful cartoon linking fun which started in 1976 before the rise of "TISWAS" and the networked Saturday morning show. As well as Lyn, her two sidekicks on the show were Malcolm Gerrie and Alastair Pirrie, both of whom would go on to be involved in pretty much every major commercial music series of the next two decades with the former going on to be executive producer on "The Tube" and "The White Room" among others. Pirrie, who sadly died in January 2017, went on to host ITV's long running 'pop and prizes' show "Razzmatazz" until 1985 and two years later became producer of "The Roxy" – one of the rare shows to attempt to try to beat "Top of the Pops" at its own game. Whilst it ultimately didn't last due to poor networking decisions and the difficulty of luring pop acts up to Newcastle it was a noble attempt and deserved a much longer run. As for Lyn Spencer herself, she left "Look In" in 1979 when she became pregnant with her first child and the name of the show was changed to "Saturday Shake-Up". She subsequently went onto host local youth series "Check It Out" and would later be reunited with Alastair Pirrie in 1981 for the first couple of series of "Razzmatazz" before being replaced by a string of hosts including one 16 year old wannabe popstar named Lisa Stansfield.

9.40am: The Sunday Gang (BBC One)

"A look at Christmas with a report from Bethlehem. with John Dryden, Jill Shakespeare, Glen Stuart and special guest Dana."

Whilst past the show's prime[13] but this lightly religious singin' and a comedyin' variety mag was a staple in the late 70s and often watched by kids just because there simply wasn't anything else to do. The hosts were a clean-cut do-good assortment of wannabe Youth Group Leaders, operating out of a clubhouse kitted out with a "computer" sporting a tape spool-hewn face with added piano keyboard, and a screeching puppet mouse called Mackintosh that called everyone 'sassenachs'. It's this mouse that Dana spends most of her time "interacting" with during this special episode from the National Children's Home in Cheshire. There's still room for some extremely boring film though however with "JD" making a trip to Tel Aviv because Christmas...and that. Plus lots and lots of unbearably over-enthusiastic singing and OVER EMOTING THE WORDS. Wake me up when it's time for "Nai Zindagi Naya Jeevan"...

5.30pm: The Beatles at Shea Stadium (BBC Two)

"By the summer of 1965, Beatlemania had become part of the British way of life; it had not yet reached the States, but The Beatles' first concert in the US, at Shea Stadium was to change all that!"

There's always been something oddly festive about The Beatles

---

[13] i.e Tina Heath had left for *Blue Peter*.

to me. It could be their four Christmas number ones or
"Magical Mystery Tour" making its TV début on Boxing Day
1967. It might even be their terrific festive fan club discs they
made, later being produced by Kenny Everett. Or perhaps it
was this season of much welcomed Beatle filmage over the
1979 holidays which gave fans a rare chance to see not just "A
Hard Day's Night" and "Help!" but lesser seen stuff; the now-
permanently vetoed Let It Be and this 50-minute quasi-
documentary containing footage from their 1965 New York
stadium concert on front of 55,000 screaming fans.

First shown on BBC One in March 1966 it also featured
extracts from the Fabs' largely soul-flavoured support acts King
Curtis, Sounds Incorporated and Brenda Holloway with dancer
and self-styled "King of the Discotheque" Killer Joe Piro. But
the material was heavily over-dubbed and partly re-recorded for
film due to the sound issues in the stadium, something not fully
revealed until the release of Ron Howard's much recommended
"The Beatles: Eight Days a Week – The Touring Years" in
2016. Shea Stadium was eventually closed in 2008 after two
final concerts by New York native and Beatle fan Billy Joel who
was fittingly joined at the end by special guest... Sir ~~Pat Sharp~~
Paul McCartney.

Tuesday, 23rd December, 1980

8.30pm: The Dawson Watch (BBC One)

"In this special edition Les takes a look at Christmas."

To me, there is no question that Les Dawson was one of the
greatest comic minds of all time with a mixture of wordplay and
character-work that wasn't given nearly enough credit in his
lifetime. He gained fame through Yorkshire TV's panel show

"Joker's Wild" and his own long-running "Sez Les" (11 series between 1969 and 1976) before he moved to the BBC. The Dawson Watch had Les embracing the (relatively) modern age with a spoof consumer programme backdrop for his sketches. Over three series, he worked with newer writers such as Andy Hamilton and Terry Ravenscroft, more commonly associated for shows like Radio 4's "Week Ending" or "Not the Nine O'Clock News". The whole series is huge fun and firmly re-established Dawson as one of the top comics of the day. This Christmas edition was the last of the three series, after which Les's work returned to more of a light entertainment tone.

9.00pm: Elvis – He Touched Their Lives (ITV)

"It is three years since the news of Elvis Presley's death flashed round the world. On what is now an annual pilgrimage, 350 members of the British Elvis Presley Fan Club go each August to pay homage. David Frost is among them as they visit the shrines in Memphis."

He touched what? Eee, the dorty sod! This documentary saw David Frost follow various fans around the haunts of Elvis' life including his old school, the Sun Studios, where he made his first acclaimed recordings, a hospital he stayed in and, of course, his grave. It comes across like a slightly more showbiz take on Louis Theroux's documentaries, never mocking its subjects but occasionally allowing them to hang themselves with their own obsessional or self-important words. There's also a wry look at the selling of Elvis's death and the near-religious fervour already surrounding his celebrity – although perhaps most shocking of all is the sight of the always on-duty Frost in a casual short-sleeved polo shirt.

Friday, 23rd December, 1983

10.25pm: An Audience with Kenneth Williams (Channel 4)

After Dame Edna Everage in 1980 and Dudley Moore in 1981, Kenneth Williams was only the third person to be awarded one of LWT's entertainment specials under the *"An Audience With"* title. There was much more to Williams than the Carry On films; he was a renowned storyteller, and one early theatre revue show – 1960's "One Over The Eight *"* – featured material by both Harold Pinter and a very young Peter Cook. The late-evening showing of An Audience With didn't bother Williams who wrote in his diary:*"Heigh ho! I don't care. The fewer viewers the better cos then I can use the material again!"* Four more "Audiences" would premiere on Channel 4: Joan Rivers (March 1984), a second one for Dame Edna Everage (December 1984), Billy Connolly (October 1985) and Jackie Mason (December 1990). The reason for this, invariably, was because of worries over the strong material, particularly in the case of Connolly whose rude set also slipped in a few F words, toxic to television in those days. But the "An Audience With" title had originally been used by a Birmingham born folk comic for his first series on ITV. Now what was his name again..?

Sunday, 23rd December, 1984

5.15pm: Jasper Carrott Got This Mole (ITV)

"A cartoon story written and told by Jasper Carrott."

…that's the feller. This was an animated version of one of Jasper's most celebrated early routines featuring the soundtrack of a sketch from his 1981 LWT special "The Unrecorded Jasper Carrott"[14].) By the time this animation by Les Gibbard had aired Jasper had moved to the BBC, reinvented himself as a topical stand-up and set his sights on conquering America. And all while suffering with this perishing mole!

10.10pm: Frank and Selina's Christmas Time (BBC One)

"Frank Bough and Selina Scott present a star-studded curtain-raiser to your Christmas viewing."

Cor, late-night naughty Selina Scott action! Okay, maybe not... sorry Dads...but it was always a huge thrill to see people you associate with one timeslot popping up in another and here was a friendly preview of BBC One's seasonal fare from the team behind Breakfast Time. Launched in January 1983, Britain's first national breakfast television series had become a surprise smash. As part of this special, presenter Mike Smith went backstage at John Sullivan's now slightly forgotten but once massive romantic sitcom "Just Good Friends" which took up a rather lengthy 90-minute section of that year's Christmas Day schedule, and paved the way for many similar feature-length adventures for the Trotter family from 1985[15]. Elsewhere Barry Norman[16] previewed the big TV films of the season. Now get to sleep you lot – Breakfast Time is on again in eight hours!

---

14 The one where he shows you what is on the other channels to prove it's live.

15 Indeed, this would be the last Christmas Day without a new episode of "Only Fools And Horses" on BBC One until 1993.

16 Norman's own "films of the year" special had aired the night before and featured Splash, The Right Stuff, Broadway Danny Rose, The Killing Fields and Romancing the Stone.

Monday, 23rd December, 1985

2.35pm: What's Up, Chuck? (BBC Two)

"Chuck Jones looks back on 50 years of cartoon-making. Today, he introduces some of his early characters – Sniffles, Hubie and Bertie and the Curious Puppies."

A positively youthful 74 in 1985, Chuck Jones is one of the most important names in animation history. Even as a kid you could see his work was vibrant, colourful and a bit more playful than some of his contemporaries although it is true that Jones outliving almost all of those meant he got the lion's share of the later celebrations, perhaps a tad unevenly. This series of ten half hour retrospectives were a huge deal to anyone interested in old cartoons and ran up to the 3rd of January with episodes focusing on different parts of Jones' work including the importance of music and sound, staging and character development. Special episodes were also devoted to his work on Bugs Bunny, Daffy Duck, Roadrunner and Wile E Coyote. And not a vetoed heavy breathing Australian in sight.

7.30pm: Sunshine Christmas (Channel 4)

"For millions the world over, Christmas is a time of warmth and sunshine. Tonight, black entertainers have created their own with a party for the stars of the black community, held at Kisses Nightspot in South London. Introduced by Rustie Lee."

A Rustie Lee party at Kisses Nightspot! I don't know what that is but it sounds like all of my hobbies and interests! The Peckham club Kisses was home at the time to a residency by the DJ Gordon Mac who decided to form a pirate radio station to play the dance and hip hop that wasn't being touched by the mainstream FM. Tying in with the nightclub, this new station would be known as Kiss FM and go legit from early 1990, eventually becoming one of Britain's biggest stations. As for Kisses, it would eventually morph into Chicago's, one of the most violent nightclubs in London before being shut down entirely. It is now a "Solution Centre" for the Crusaders Ministries International. Whatever that means.

Tuesday, 23rd December, 1986

9.00pm: Moonlighting (BBC Two)

"What does Christmas mean to the people at Blue Moon? For Maddie, it's a time of warmth and giving – but not to Addison! For David, it's an opportunity to initiate 'Santa's Hotline' and get that little extra in his stocking..."

It's fair to say that quirky comic detective series "Moonlighting" was something of a revolution when it first hit America's ABC network in March 1985. It boasted witty scripts, a perfectionist creator – Glenn Gordon Caron – who aimed to make a mini-movie each week and an amazing cast headed by the fast-talking Cybill Shepherd and Bruce Willis, rebooting and starting their careers respectively. Here in the UK, its feature-length pilot appeared in May 1986 on BBC One with the series itself continuing three days later on BBC Two. To catch up with America and the already huge demand, they ran the first and second seasons almost in full back-to-back by the time the third came around in the US. Held back for obvious reasons though was "'Twas the Episode Before Christmas" which finds Willis's character David convinced he's trapped in a festive allegory; Biblical tinged events like characters called Joseph and Mary looking for a baby and a visit from three (i.e. men with the same surname) Kings. The episode's odd conclusion comes when the cast suddenly work out they are in a Christmas episode: it begins to snow inside the office and carollers start to sing. On leaving the office they walk onto the set where to discover the musical accompaniment is from the crew of Moonlighting before breaking the fourth wall to wish everyone at home Merry Christmas. Okay, it sounds awful but I promise it's quite sweet. Now, Christmas Eve in Nakatomi Plaza on the other hand...

Wednesday, 23rd December, 1987

9.30pm: The Home-Made Xmas Video (BBC Two)

"A Video de Dad. It's full of lots of things about Christmas. What we did, where we went, what we ate, how much we all drunk and everything. It's a great stuff! (The turkey, I mean.) But seriously..."

No Christmas period for me is properly started until I've seen this spin-off from the later series of "Alas Smith and Jones" which took an affectionate but honest look at British working class families via the new-fangled home camcorder. There's well-meaning but quick to temper Dad (Jones), happy but put upon Mum (Diane Langton), kids Shirley and Peter (Jenny Jay and Nigel Harman) and their fun, illiterate and frequently drunk lodger Len (Smith) who almost anticipates the character of Homer Simpson. Sequences involving simple acts like putting a wreath on the door, badly stealing a tree and visiting sick relatives are made into painfully funny sequences that are never played cheaply for cringe laughs. Likewise the family are rough but never sneered at by Griff and Robin Driscoll's script which makes them fully rounded likeable characters and could easily have been spun off into a full series. Mel and Griff's wonderful BBC Two swansong "Alas Sage And Onion" sadly just misses out on featuring in this book due to airing on 21st December 1988 which also happened to be the same night as the crash of Pan Am flight 103 onto the Scottish town of Lockerbie. The news broke just before that special went to air and viewers may not have been ready to be greeted straight after by a Beverley Sisters parody and a shot of the pair supposedly hanging from tinsel nooses[17].

Friday, 23rd December, 1988

5.00pm: Billy's Christmas Angels (BBC One)

"Billy wants to play in a rock band with his brother Dave. 'Dreams' says Dad. So Billy's Angels come down to earth to help find Dave – and reality – through Faith, Hope & 'Charlie'..."

A single half-hour Liverpudlian pop fantasy with stunning music from the British six-piece a capella group and former Stiff Records signings The Mint Juleps who play the titular angels. Staged like a kitchen sink drama initially before veering off into more fantastical realms, Billy clashes with his harsh but sensible parents who don't want him to run off like his older brother. Inevitably he does and bumps into the always welcome Daniel Peacock as the Disney villain-esque Mr Big and his henchman Steve Johnson, who seems incredibly out of place to those who remember him later on as part of ITV's

---

17 Luckily a quickie sketch about disastrous Greek air traffic control was removed just before broadcast.

"Motormouth" presenting team. Later, Nabil Shaban appears as a philosophising junk shop owner and the story meanders to some sort of conclusion with the brothers reuniting and a lesson probably being learnt by somebody. It all lacks the charm of similar BBC shows of the era and exists now purely to torment people who can only half-remember what it was. Also the kid playing Billy is bloody awful. Nice music, though.

7.00pm: Christmas Telly Addicts (BBC One)

"Join Noel for a Christmas clash of the TV titans."

Noel Edmonds continues his jackbooted and garishly jumpered domination of our late Decembers with the still much-missed TV quiz. Competing were "The Cotton Club", a team comprising of the BBC Managing Director Bill Cotton with Terry Wogan, Tim Rice and TV critic Margaret Forwood and opponents "The Gradey Bunch" aka new Channel 4 chief Michael Grade with Ernie Wise, Susan Reynish from 1986's winning "Telly Addicts" family plus a seemingly unannounced Leslie Grantham whose appearance seems to throw the usually unflappable Noel for the first few minutes. The regular quiz then continues as normal until near the end of the show[18] when some comedy police officers appear on set – again apparently without Noel's prior knowledge – to arrest 'Dirty Den'[19] Of course everyone – ho ho! - naturally points at Noel who is cuffed and carted off by the fuzz never to be seen again. It's basically Rodney King in bad knitwear.

---

18 The Gradey Bunch won 27-24. Noel wears a horrific Adidas branded jumper throughout. So, ultimately, nobody wins.

19 Grantham's EastEnders character who at the time was in jail eventually being "killed off" in 1989.

9.30pm: Blackadder's Christmas Carol (BBC One)

"Christmas Eve, 1850. Ebenezer Blackadder is a decent, kind, generous human being. As far as his loathsome ancestors are concerned, he is a wrong 'un. So, as soon as he is snuggled up in bed they decide to pay him a visit. A seasonal tale of almost unbearable cuteness."

Reworking the character of Blackadder, established as a vicious scheming bastard over three prior series, "Blackadder's Christmas Carol" is a superb reverse re-treading of the Dickens tale as a sketch show for various incarnations of the Adder dynasty. Viewers of more recent repeats, however, have been denied one of the funniest lines from the original broadcast. Blackadder and Baldrick are discussing the workhouse's production of the Nativity being hindered the high infant mortality rate and so a dog named Spot is instead made the saviour of all humanity (*"I'm not convinced that Christianity would have established its firm grip over the hearts and minds of all mankind if all Jesus had ever said was 'woof'..."*) A despairing Blackadder asks if the children were upset but quite the contrary: *"...They loved it. They want us to do another one at Easter. They want to see us nail up the dog."*

Jem Roberts' excellent book "The True History of the Blackadder" (Random House, 2012) has producer John Lloyd very down on the line saying: "It's breathtakingly cruel and very dark. And you don't just get the Jesus lobby, you've got the dog lobby as well!" which could explain its later disappearance from TV and Region 2 DVDs.

("The Black Hole of Calcutta is currently appearing in Baldrick's trousers.")

1.00am: The James Whale Radio Show (ITV)

"Conversational Humorous Risque Irreverent Stimulating Topical Musical Argumentative Suggestive! Progressive Absurd Raunchy Titillating Yuletide! Call us on 0532 461000 and join in."

It's over to the studios of Radio Aire for a "Christmas Party", an hour of live, challenging and, most importantly, cheap TV. In fairness to James Whale he's personable, self-mocking and in control throughout the show – at one point a man in cricket gear fully blacked-up walks on and sits with the guests to their clear surprise – but it's a strange ill-fitting mixture of a programme that features a serious filmed report on "should the police be armed?" next to lingerie-clad women, drunk callers and an interview with a visibly unimpressed Stan Boardman making jokes about "willy woofters". It was post-pub TV writ large and probably what the audience actually wanted to see back then but when was the public ever right about anything? A show perhaps best summed up by Fist of Fun's Peter Baynham: *"And then a lady comes on in just her bra and James Whale smiles."*

Saturday, 23rd December, 1989

10.20am: The Batman (Channel 4)

"Bruce Wayne, outwardly a rich and idle playboy, is in reality America's deadliest crimefighter.

With the first Tim Burton film becoming the second highest grossing film of the year[20], Channel 4 took the opportunity to

---

20 Behind Indiana Jones and the Last Crusade.

repeat this series of creaky 1943 cinema shorts that put the Dynamic Duo on screen for the very first time, four years after Batman burst into existence in that now somewhat valuable issue of Detective Comics #27. Unusually, the 'chapter play drama' doesn't contain any of his famous back catalogue of classic villains but an evil Japanese agent (yes, it's incredibly racist. Don't you know there was a war on...?) called Dr. Daka who wants to steal the city's radium to power a hand-held laser ray for various nefarious baddie style reasons. Also here Bats is a secret government agent as opposed to a bitter vigilante. The 1949 sequel series "Batman and Robin" appeared on Channel 4 the following Christmas.

Wednesday, 23rd December, 1992

9.30pm: Lenny Henry: In Dreams (BBC One)

"A comic fantasy which takes a sideways, quizzical look into the world of dreams and nightmares."

An awkward but entertaining one-off vehicle in which Bill Paterson plays a therapist delving into Henry's subconscious allowing Len to investigate stranger avenues of comedy often connected to very real fears in the comic's life. One such sketch sees him crush three unpleasant newspaper hacks under his actually growing gargantuan bot. Later Barry Norman pops up to critique his acting in a short film about going to the toilet titled "Bastard". Coming the year after Len's flop big break movie in the US "True Identity" the bruises were very real and still clearly sore. I still think it's quite good myself.

December 24th

It's beginning to look a lot like wossname!

Yes, its Christmas Eve! You can now officially kick off your work trousers and replace them with your special festive pants. If all has gone to plan your freshly wrapped presents are safe to put under the tree, the unspeakably huge amounts of food are being prepared and far too much booze has been purchased… because Christmas is for the kiddies really, innit?

You might be travelling to a loved one's house to spend the holiday with them although this tends to lack the romance you see in American films as its less about mad dashing to make a date than being stuck on the M25 listening to Steve Wright play "Driving Home For Christmas" without any trace of irony for the umpteenth bloody time.

Whatever happens, it's time to let go of the cynicism and concentrate on what really matters in this ever so short life that we spend on this Earth: Television! And going out for that sneaky pint is put to the test when TV properly steps up its game and starts putting on the stuff you actually wouldn't mind seeing. The shows and films that might be a bit too rude for the big day itself when Grandma and troubled Aunt Susan with the weeping ~~bum~~ eye might be watching. Every sitcom and predictable panel show has ten minutes stapled on to its usual length and there's a nice long film taking full advantage of the fact the news doesn't have to be on directly at 10pm.

Blimey! It might actually be Christmas after all…

Thursday, 24th December, 1964

6.35pm: Mister Magoo's Christmas Carol (BBC One)

Considered to be the first full length Christmas cartoon made specifically for TV, this was originally shown by NBC in December 1962 and found the comically short sighted character playing the role of Scrooge on stage. Largely forgotten in the UK but still a big staple of the American TV schedule each Christmas the animation here remains gorgeous, vibrant and colourful. Of note is that the special not only uses many of Dickens original words but also contains original songs by Jule Styne and Bob Merrill whose new musical Funny Girl would open on Broadway the following year to huge success later spawning an even more successful 1968 movie adaptation. But did it have a mostly blind man falling over a bin or driving the wrong way into a tunnel? Possibly. I haven't seen it.

7.25pm: Top of the Pops '64 (BBC One)

The first ever "Pops" Christmas special documented one of the most exciting years in pop ever with The Supremes, The Kinks, Sandie Shaw, The Animals, Manfred Mann and – of course – The Beatles Band all taking the stage. "Top Of The Pops" would move to Christmas Day the following year at 10.35pm but would not attain its traditional pre-Queen slot until 1967. However, BBC One's "Christmas Night With The Stars" – a cornucopia of newly filmed clips from various hit series – did award five minutes on Christmas Day 1964 to the smash hit new pop show. They were filled by The Barron Knights mocking the bands of the time with Christmas themed lyrics. More on that bunch later in the book. Although not later enough for some...

Saturday, 24th December, 1966

7.50pm: I Gotta Shoe (BBC Two)

"...or Cindy-Ella. Written by Caryl Brahms and Ned Sherrin."

Merry jazzmas everybody! Making it to TV after initially being commissioned as a radio piece for the Home Service in 1957, this mixture of Cinderella and songs from the American Deep South had been performed at London's Garrick Theatre four years earlier. For this hour long adaptation, that same cast reunited, headed by Cleo Laine whose voice was already well known thanks to many appearances on BBC Radio's Light Programme with her husband Johnny Dankworth, plus regular Sunday night slots on "Not So Much a Programme, More a Way of Life" also devised by Ned Sherrin.

Sunday, 24th December, 1967

5.50pm: How the Grinch Stole Christmas (BBC Two)

"Boris Karloff narrates this unusual and amusing Christmas story"

Another US animated classic that really does stand up to lots of re-watching thanks to the gorgeous artwork directed by Chuck Jones, memorable music ("You're A Mean One Mr Grinch" performed by Thurl Ravenscroft) and perfectly pitched narration from Boris Karloff. Lesser known are the follow ups "Halloween Is Grinch Night" from 1977 and 1982's big name Seuss showdown crossover event "The Grinch Grinches the Cat in the Hat" in which the green git is generally a bit of a pain in the arse to the fancy-chapeaued feline for half an hour.

Tuesday, 24th December, 1968

7.25pm: The Gang Show (BBC One)

"Excerpts from the 1968 production with a cast of 120 of the Scout & Guide Movement recorded at The Odeon, Golders Green."

The sixties are credited with a lot of change, from gay rights to breaking racial tensions but it was peanuts compared to 1968 when the The Gang Show's traditional all-male cast was bolstered by the appearance of...gulp...women!....as the Scout Association invited members of the Girl Guides Association and Girl Scout leaders to take part. And to quote the Radio Times: *"The girls have made a terrific impact. Their standard was so high that one of the leading singers has been offered a professional contract as principal girl in a London pantomime."* See? Being nice to females is a good idea, not bad like you and Skeletor thought.

Wednesday, 24th December, 1969

1.50pm: 1969 – Year of Space (BBC One)

"Patrick Moore who surveys the space highlights and astronomical achievements of 1969."

Space was all the rage in '69 thanks to them American chaps stomping all over the moon and the BBC was right along with them with live footage on the night that July plus this "The Sky At Night" special. And a much more suitable special than the alternative specials they could've planned: "1969 – Year of Midnight Cowboy Coming Out", "1969 – Year of Dominik Diamond Being Born" or "1969 – Year of Charles Manson".

Wednesday, 24th December, 1969

9.15pm: Carry on Christmas (ITV)

Thursday, 24th December, 1970

9.10pm: Carry on Again Christmas (ITV)

Depending on your view, 1969 either saw the Carry On films series peaking at the box office with "Carry On Camping" and "Carry On Again, Doctor" both released that year; or dragging on with increasingly less subtlety or joy as the ever-aging cast go through the motions for money yet again. To give credence to the latter, as well as the two cinema releases, 1969 was the first year it was decided to bring the team to Thames TV for an adaptation of A Christmas Carol with Sid James as Scrooge. Also a strange sub-plot about Terry Scott as Dr. Frank N. Stein and Peter Butterworth as his assistant Dracula. The special was one of ITV's most popular shows of Christmas week meaning a 1970 follow up was inevitable. This time round it was a Treasure Island pastiche with cabin boy played by a woman! (Barbara Windsor naturally.) The Carry On films will outlast all of us. This is their world, we just live in it.

Friday, 24th December, 1971

6.55pm: Christmas! What's It All About? (BBC Two)

"Questionmaster Brian Redhead with an audience of schoolchildren in which you are invited to compete against Jimmy Savile OBE..."

No.

Monday, 24th December, 1973

5.15pm: The Goodies and the Beanstalk (BBC Two)

"The Goodies barter their most valuable possession for some beans and get more than they bargained for."

A hugely entertaining attack on pantomimes and the clichés that come with them, this special is only slightly pipped in quality by their 1974 special "The Goodies Rule – O.K?" which unleashed the giant marauding Dougal from "The Magic Roundabout" into pop culture history. The Beeb later chose this episode in 1983 to be released to the home market as one of the earliest comedy titles on the BBC Video label. Due to the cost[21] of tapes it wasn't a huge seller and no more BBC Goodies episodes would appear until 1994. The series as a whole features a number of playful digs at their friends in "Monty Python" but this special is the only one to actually feature one of the cast thanks to a cameo by John Cleese as a genie announcing *"And now for something completely different"*. When told to push off he heckles them with *"KID'S PROGRAMME!"* acknowledging the subversive appeal of The Goodies' to a young audience.

Tuesday, 24th December, 1974

7.45pm: The Likely Lads (BBC One)

"Bob and Thelma are determined to enjoy the Christmas festivities to the full but, inevitably, Terry creates a problem or two for Bob which starts the season off on quite the wrong foot."

---

[21] Average tapes around the time sold between £40 and £60.

Ohhhhh, what happened to you? Despite the Radio Times titling this was the final episode of "Whatever Happened to the Likely Lads?" which leaves the series in a very strange space as an utterly bored and newly-bearded Bob spends the entire episode trying to shag someone who isn't his wife while a perfectly amiable Terry gets a job as a mini cab driver. It's a very funny episode but the farcical elements mean much of the subtle nature of the preceding 26 episodes is lost. The theme tune gets a nice jingle bell makeover though.

Saturday, 24th December, 1977

9.40pm: Bing Crosby's Merrie Olde Christmas (ITV)

"Bing's last show, recorded just before his death, features his family, music, laughter, a touch of Dickens and of course White Christmas"

Well, I'm glad they didn't record it after his death as that would've been really tough to shoot. This is the show that gave the world that awkward but hugely enjoyable Bing and Bowie duet, which had been apparently concocted at the last minute when the latter didn't fancy a performing a straight take of "Little Drummer Boy". There's also Scottish comedian Stanley Baxter playing the entire staff of Bing's long-lost English relative Sir Percival Crosby, most of them bearing a passing resemblance to the characters of ITV's drama "Upstairs Downstairs" which had been a huge hit on both sides of the Atlantic. There's also Ron Moody and Twiggy as various characters including Charles Dickens and Tiny Tim. Despite the inherent naffness, the special is actually quite sweet and you'd never assume Crosby was five weeks away from the grave with that spectacular voice in great form throughout.

Sunday, 24th December, 1978

3.15pm: Emmet Otter's Jug-Band Christmas (ITV)

"Jim Henson, creator of the world-famous Muppets, presents a one-hour Christmas special with Emmet Otter and his friends..."

"Emmet Otter's Jug-Band Christmas", based on Russell Hoban's 1971 children's tale of the same name and introduced by Kermit the Frog,[22] is beautiful, touching, funny, ridiculous and full of terrific new Paul Williams songs and perfect for giving you the warm fuzzies...which is apt for when you're watching a bunch of warm fuzzies, I suppose. Emmet and his mother Alice live a poor life in an old shack barely getting by doing odd jobs until each of them notices that a big prize talent contest is happening and decides to surprise the other by entering. Originally shown by HBO in December 1977, its quaint but there's a more anarchic side too when their town is over-run by teenage menaces who later form – with a hat-tip to Alice Cooper – The Riverbottom Nightmare Band.

5.20pm: Pinocchio (BBC One)

"Betrayed to the evil wagon driver by Mr Fox and Mr Cat, Pinocchio has departed with his school-fellows for the Land of Toys."

A world away from the cuddly fun of the Muppets is this 1978 adaptation of Pinocchio – already quite a bleak story by Carlo

---

22 Unless you're watching the Region 2 DVD release from 2011 where the bits with Kermit setting the story up are completely snipped out for some reason. He was returned for the 40th anniversary edition.

Collodi in which a naughty marionette is hanged from a tree and killed – which scarred many young viewers at the time. This was mostly because of the dead-eyed and oft-screeching puppet which interacted with real human actors thanks to the best BBC visual effects available at the time. Thankfully for all those scared kids, this was the final episode of the "Sunday Classics" adaptation and it was all over bar the thousands of cleaning bills the BBC got sent for a nation's sodden junior mattresses on Baby Jesus's birthday. That is until 1987 and The Two Ronnies' "Pinocchio II – Killer Doll"...

Thursday, 24th December, 1981

7.45pm: The Kenny Everett Television Show (BBC One)

"This is Kenny Everett's first show for the BBC and in it he will be doing several things we're not allowed to talk about and meeting several people we're not at liberty to divulge. Suffice it to say, everything will be completely original in as much as it's never been done before... on the BBC. Join Kenny and the cast of thousands for the experience of a lifetime. Or, on the other hand, watch this show."

To say that Kenny Everett joining the BBC was something akin to placing a stick of dynamite in a nice vase of petunias wouldn't be far off the truth. Leaving previous employers Thames after they scheduled him against "Top of the Pops" despite them sharing the exact same audience, Everett's appearances on Auntie Beeb were perhaps slicker but no less exciting and fully of genuine naughty bits. This first half-hour for the BBC is a perfect calling card beginning with spinning newspapers revealing his defection (*"Biggest betrayal since Pearl Harbour!"* – *Daily Mail*, *"Who Cares?"* – *Gay News*) followed by some black and white faux-horror movie footage of Ev being bundled out of a car marked "ITV1" and buried in a shallow grave before being dug up again by two BBC chaps in a clapped out Austin. With this, Everett fired warning shots at both sides AND mocked his own place in the showbusiness world – and all in the first 40 seconds! Much like his previous Thames shows there are cut-out animations, familiar characters, a set full of television screens and no studio audience yet but bags of confidence from the get go. Plus it's very, very funny. A memorable running sketch finds Ken wandering the corridors of the much-missed BBC TV Centre explaining what all the initials on the doors mean ("DG: Director General", "OB OPS: Outside Broadcast Operators"). He then assumes "BUM" must naturally stand for "Broadcasting Under Manager" but is instead, terrifically, a giant bottom which later blasts Terry Wogan through a nearby wall. There's also a look at the cobwebbed BBC Boardroom as decrepit old executives try to work out the appeal of Everett, an episode of crass American-style game show called "Shoot The Dog" and guest stars The Police, Billy Connolly and David Frost who crops up to point out a sketch has been ripped off from his own 1960s show "The Frost Report". Plus the first appearance of the never ashamed US actress Cupid Stunt. And of course it's all done...

Monday, 24th December, 1984

3.45pm: Telly Quiz (BBC Two)

"Jerry Stevens asks Easy, Medium or Hard. They're the category of questions in this quiz all about television. See how many programmes you can remember from the Coronation to the present day."

4.15pm: Pop Quiz Christmas Special (BBC One)

"As the family covers the Dansette in tinsel Mike Read hosts a special edition of the musical trivia game with seasonal goodies from the archives."

It's a double bill of quizzes meaning double the opportunity for a family argument! YAY! First up is the simply-titled and utterly forgotten pre-"Telly Addicts" TV trivia quiz that ran the full length of Christmas 1984. Then it's a change of channel and a seasonal instalment of "Pop Quiz" with calypso king Mike Read overseeing the truly baffling teams of Noddy Holder, Toyah and a clearly desperate Meat Loaf versus Queen's Roger Taylor, Brian "Nasher" Nash from Frankie Goes to Hollywood and Green Gartside of Scritti Politti. Despite being a staple of Saturday nights, heavily merchandised and long associated with the eighties, few could guess "Pop Quiz" was only four days from its final BBC One episode – a legendary showdown between Duran Duran and Spandau Ballet. Clearly thinking that was the peak of all human endeavours the show stopped, giving time for Read to concentrate on his true passions – radio and writing mildly xenophobic pop songs. Joy.

5.35pm: The Box of Delights (BBC One)

"The last of six episodes. Kay is trapped in the dungeons below. Can he find his magic box and prevent Abner's terrible plans?"

Much like "Pinocchio" a few pages back, 1984's "The Box of Delights" is an adaptation of a classic children's story brought to life on TV with the latest state-of-the-art graphics. However, rather than bloody terrifying, instead it's rather a charming period piece with visuals that have obviously dated now, because of their reliance on green screen and Chroma key – but were a huge innovation at the time. Despite being produced as a play for radio many times, John Masefield's 1935 story was thought unfilmable for many years with sequences featuring characters escaping into moving paintings or being miniaturised by the titular box but the full might of the BBC's design, costume and visual effects departments did it proud. Admittedly, the graphics don't look that much compared to today's CGI effects but they suit the production entirely and provided much excitement when previewed on the likes of "Saturday Superstore" and "Blue Peter" and have a realistic, pleasingly solid feel unlike Superman throwing a thousand Batmans into a digital skyscraper. Disbelief is also helped by a well-chosen cast including the wonderful Patrick Troughton as mysterious Cole Hawlings who has a secret that accidentally drags a young man and his friends into adventure. Its legacy is so dependable that several people I know still watch their DVD as individual episodes on the original dates it went out on in 1984, using it almost as a televisual advent calendar. Come along Barney dog...

8.00pm: Jim Davidson's Falklands Special (ITV)

"A unique film follows the British entertainer 8,000 miles to the South Atlantic, which, two years ago, was a scene of conflict. From Ascension Island to Goose Green Jim entertains the men and women of the armed forces, many of whom will not be home for Christmas."

The sort of manipulative "our brave boys" guff that ITV are still secretly fond of featuring a comedian they couldn't get enough of with his harmless but charmless sitcoms "Up the

Elephant and Round the Castle" and its sequel "Home James" being on screen for just under a decade. Thames followed this Falklands spectacular up two years later with another Christmas Eve programme entitled "Jim Davidson in Germany" in which he once again met some soldiers whose leave did not correspond with this festive period. Only this time he took Richard Digance as well. Thanks for nothing Galtieri...

Wednesday, 24th December, 1986

2.00pm: Pob's Christmas Special (Channel 4)

"Ice, wind and snow blow through Pob's Programme today but there's lots of Christmas cheer as well. A special present for Dick King-Smith and a party poem from Su Pollard."

For a programme so utterly beloved by its core audience and a huge part of the early success behind kids TV behemoth Ragdoll Productions, there's barely a scrap of "Pob's Programme" anywhere in the Internet. Yet for a generation that jaunty parping theme tune, celebrities following unravelling coloured jumper strings to rhyming clues, Dick King Smith's boring inserts with his dog, the "naughty teddy" and Pob "cleaning" the end credits off the inside of your TV screen are etched in the mind vividly. As for the guest Su Pollard, she'd been clearing up that Christmas with appearances at that year's Royal Variety Performance, "A Question Of Sport" and, of course, on Hi-de-Hi! which would come to the end of its eighth and penultimate series on December 27th, 1986. Meanwhile her début album "Su" featuring her no. 2 hit "Starting Together" reached a trouser-shattering number 86 in the UK album charts. What would Miss Cathcart say?!?

Sunday, 24th December, 1989

9.00pm: One Hour with Jonathan Ross (Channel 4)

"Jonathan cooks up a seasonal feast of music, laughter and chat from which the giblets have been carefully removed."

Now largely forgotten after Jonathan's previous chat show "The Last Resort" had been a huge success for Channel 4, this bigger-scale live Sunday night production did give valuable early air time to a number of great comic minds including Charlie Higson, Paul Whitehouse, Kathy Burke, Vic Reeves and Bob Mortimer, most of whom were used as part of a strange game show named "Knock Down Ginger", the seeds of which wouldn't be a million miles away from "Shooting Stars" several years later[23]. Indeed, Vic and Bob's humour is a strong influence throughout much of the series' tone which could explain the British public's general indifference. The series was pushed back mid-run to "The Last Resort"'s old timeslot on Fridays 10:30pm.. It changed very little and Ross decided to cut his losses and move on to the only slightly more memorable "Tonight with Jonathan Ross" at teatimes instead.

Monday, December 24th, 1990

5:45pm: Billy the Fish (Channel 4)

"Billy realises his dream to play in goal for Fulchester United and rises to stardom in the battle against arch rivals, Grimethorpe City."

---

[23] Ross was even team captain on the "Shooting Stars" pilot (See "At Home With Vic and Bob" entry)

"Ooookay Billy, yew can gaw in gawelll...." Missing the "Viz being fashionable" wave by an inch, Channel 4 nonetheless played a blinder when it was suggested that "Billy the Fish" and Fulchester United's increasingly ridiculous footballing adventures could be made into five minute daily cartoons to coincide with the World Cup finals in June 1990, compiled as an omnibus here. The half man, half fish keeper first appeared in issue 10 of Viz, as a pastiche the football strips with strange premises in "boys papers" of the fifties & sixties and a perfect choice as, unlike much of the comic's stock in trade, the strip rarely contained bad language, violence or other unsuitable behaviour for teatime. Due to the idea only being mooted in March 1990 the race was on to find someone quick and, more importantly, cheap enough to produce the shorts on time. It led Channel 4 to the door of Tony Barnes from Fairwater Films in Cardiff best known at the time for making gentle ITV cartoon "The Shoe People".

Using the original comic strip text as the script and the voice talents of friend to the Viz team[24] Harry Enfield as...well, everybody, the cartoons are rough but spirited and the modest budget somehow adds to the charm of Billy and his team's strange world. This broadcast was a warm up to "The Further Adventures Of Billy The Fish" which began the following day. Channel 4 would later try out another Viz favourite, "Roger Mellie – The Man on the Telly" with the foul mouthed TV star voiced perfectly by the legendary Peter Cook, although the more adult content meant they didn't want any more with "The Fat Slags" and "Sid The Sexist" declared to be too rude for telly and remaining exclusive to video.

---

[24] Enfield had contacted them in 1988 about writing material for Loadsamoney's Northern counterpart Buggerallmoney on Channel 4's "Friday Night Live". He still couldn't do the accent, mind.

6.00pm: A Grand Day Out (Channel 4)

"Where is the most obvious place to find cheese? With a home-made rocket, Wallace and Gromit set off on an adventure to the Moon."

And the animation continues, although this one took somewhat longer to complete than "Billy The Fish"; Nick Park's painstakingly produced student film was first started in 1982 and only completed in 1989. Even Peter Sallis had completely forgotten he'd recorded his part for it. Though we often associate this cheese-chomping pair with the BBC, it was Channel 4 who first introduced us to them with this broadcast. "A Grand Day Out" was nominated for Best Animated Short Film at the 1990 Academy Awards but was sadly beaten by "Creature Comforts" made by...um, Nick Park. Wallace and Gromit have since always been part of Christmas it feels with the follow up film "The Wrong Trousers" airing on Boxing Day 1993 and "A Close Shave" receiving a huge amount of promotion ahead of its Christmas Eve 1995 premiere on BBC Two, with the duo even appearing on the channel's animated festive idents that year. Cracking.

Thursday, December 24th, 1992

9.20pm: Harry Enfield's Festive Television Programme (BBC Two)

The final BBC Two appearance for some time by Enfield who was primed to upgrade to the main channel with his "Chums". It's a hell of a send-off though with the Old Gits running "Santa's Grotty", Lee and Lance discussing the point of The

Queen and whether she should be replaced by Bob Monkhouse. There's also an incredibly depressing-in-the-current-climate Party Political Broadcast explaining The Maastrict Treaty and the point of being in "YERP". The best is saved for last however when Smashie and Nicey take to the hospital as they do a lot of great work for charity but don't like to "sing about it" before performing a magnificent and self-aggrandizing overblown ballad (*"I can't walk past a / natural disaster / no-one's there faster / with signed photographs / I turn up quite 'liderally' / at every catastrophe / I've saved humanity / on your behalf"*.) A perfect end to one of the great sketch shows that people still quote even 25 years on. As Dave Nice might say, "Bum tiddle tiddle bum tiddle tiddle bum bum bum bum."

10.00pm: The Comic Strip Presents... (BBC Two)

"Wild Turkey - Jim and Sue buy an unplucked turkey and discover to their horror that it is far from dead. The bird takes them hostage and demands the release of all turkeys."

A largely joke-free special from The Comic Strip team (though only Jennifer Saunders and co-writer Peter Richardson are present from the original line-up) after two great one-offs earlier in 1992; a biopic spoof of John Major entitled "Red Nose Of Courage" and Keith Allen's surprisingly great football drama "The Crying Game". This seasonal production does however feature the appearance of a brand new Kate Bush song – the gorgeous "Home For Christmas" – which would be her second for a Comic Strip film following her tribute to Ken Livingstone (simply entitled "Ken") from 1990's "GLC: the Carnage Continues".

December 25th

Waking from his terrible dream, Ebenezer Holder knew there was no time to spare and ran to the nearest window. Spying a young boy passing, he flung open and shouted down to the child *"ITS CHRIIIISSSSTMMMMASSSSSSSSSSS!"* And wouldn't you believe it, he's right an' all.

We all have our own ways and rituals to spend the big day - be it with family, friends or alone with a copy of the Freeman's catalogue and a tub of Swarfega. There'll most likely be an indecent amount of food available and even a few gifts to open. But we all know what really matters: the true meaning of Christmas... is there anything actually worth watching on the box?

What's the big film? Is there a Bond on? How many Shreks are there? Will this be the year you finally don't know any of the songs on this year's *Top of the Pops*? How many times will Mrs Brown fall over and say "feck"? Who are any of these people in the soaps you haven't watched since last Christmas Day? Why is Keith Lemon being paid? How many times will Great Aunt Florrie ask which one is William Hartnell? And will this finally be the year The Queen breakdances?

Of course now it doesn't really matter thanks to catch up services and yer Netflixes and Amazon Primes and Ian Youtubes and that, you can watch whatever whenever. And yet there's still a part of all of us that secretly quite enjoys returning to the days of being stuck in front of whatever happens to be on with your loved ones. It's a tradition that has existed since the cathode ray tube first squeezed its way down the chimney, or some other confused analogy about Christmas TV.

Let's check to see if those memories stand up, shall we?

Wednesday, 25th December, 1963

9.30am: Her Majesty The Queen (BBC One)

"A sound recording of The Queen's Christmas message."

All stand for our first entry as we start with a Christmas Day biggie which actually seems to make more sense at half 9 than it does at 3pm and not just because it's easier to kip through. It's a Liz-branded jolt before the day starts proper before people are too stuffed or plastered to take in the words. Whilst the Royal Christmas Message had been televised since 1957, this 1963 speech had reverted back to audio only due to The Queen being six months pregnant with Prince Edward. The main subject here was about helping to lessen world hunger and *"the need for humanity to be ambitious for the achievement of what is good and honourable"* which is a bit of a let-down after 1962 which was all about going to space and the launch of Telstar. Here's hoping she mentions 4K virtual reality robo-trousers this year! Or at least doesn't die before this book comes out...

Friday, 25th December, 1964

4.10pm: Disney Time (BBC One)

Cor! The first ever "Disney Time" at Christmas! And it's presented by Shary Bobbins herself, Ms. Julie Andrews whose new film "Mary Poppins" was less than a week old in UK cinemas at the time. Another staple of any holiday for decades; "Disney Time" offered a rare pre-VHS chance to see bits from varied House of Mouse productions, both animated and live-action, when Disney was the exclusive domain of the cinemas.

This edition featured an eclectic mix with the famous ("Lady and the Tramp", "Peter Pan") with the markedly less so ("The Legend of Lobo", "Those Calloways") Subsequent editions, often twice a year with a second programme at Easter or on a bank holiday, would be less arsed how connected to Disney the presenter was with French cabaret star Maurice Chevalier stepping up next, followed by the dart-in-a-board casting likes of Val Doonican (1968), Harry Worth (1969), Paul and Linda McCartney (1973), Derek Nimmo (1974), Marti Caine (1980), Windsor Davies (1981), Jan Francis (1985) and Kenny Everett (1987). The very final edition in 1995 was hosted by Michaela Strachan who fittingly saw in the next age of animation with a preview of "Toy Story". To infinity and the other one!

Saturday, 25ᵗʰ December, 1965

6.35pm: Doctor Who – The Feast of Steven (BBC One)

"The Doctor spends Christmas in a Station, and Steven misses his big chance."

When "Doctor Who" returned to our screens in 2005 it was a real punch-the-air celebration - the fact that it was really good too seemed almost secondary. But even more exciting was the announcement after Christopher Eccleston had regenerated into a slightly cheaper actor that the show would be back on Christmas Day. No longer was the series the shame of the station but smack bang in the centre of their plans for the biggest telly day of the year! Prior to 2005 this was an event that only happened once before and then only really because December 25ᵗʰ fell on Who's regularly scheduled day. That episode was "The Feast of Steven" which appeared in the middle of the exciting 12-part spectacular "The Daleks' Master Plan" which is now almost entirely missing from the archives.

Newcomers to the series, however, did not need to be up to speed on the plot though as the nail-biting action of the serial was put on hold for a week with the cast instead having some knockabout fun. First they visit a 1960s police station[25] then pop over to a Hollywood film studio for a pastiche of silent movie comedies, complete with caption cards and plinky plonky piano. With 20 minutes safely farted away the team return to the TARDIS where they realise its Christmas Day and, when in a move quite common at the time but slightly cringe-worthy now, William Hartnell turns to the camera to say *"...and a Merry Christmas to all of you at home!"* An odd episode but at least you didn't have to try and explain the plot twelve times to an elderly relative like the modern ones.

Wednesday, 25th December, 1968

4.10pm: Do Not Adjust Your Stocking (ITV)

"As you relax, glass in hand, comfortably filled with Christmas pudding and your paper hat at a rakish angle, all seems well with the world. There are, however, one or two little questions which gnaw at the aura of mellowness which surrounds you. Admit it – you want to know what was in Denise Coffey's Christmas stocking, how Captain Fantastic coped with his shopping and where Father Christmases go in the summertime. This programme gives you the answers to these and other vital questions."

---

25 Initially meant to be the police station occupied by fellow BBC One drama *Z Cars* but vetoed by spoilsports in management.

A special, extended Christmas edition of the "Fairly Pointless Show" best known now for its part in the creation of the Monty Python team. I wonder what kids thought in 1969 when they saw the names of their childhood teatime heroes – Michael Palin, Terry Jones and Eric Idle – next to some weirdly titled circus show at 11 o'clock on a Sunday night. "Do Not Adjust Your Set" was one of those quintessential "rush home from work to see it" shows usually scheduled around 5:20pm and, in some regions, slightly later repeats were added for those poor pin-striped, bowler hatted chaps stuck on buses wishing they were watching the latest episode of "Captain Fantastic". As for the series itself it's a cheap and cheerful sketch show for kids that much like the Pythons' later work, revels in wordplay and confounding expectations with Denise Coffey capable of playing any comic type and the diminutive David Jason frequently the frequently flustered foil and brilliant at it.[26]

This Christmas Day special features the extravagant, colourful (even in black and white!) and always fascinating Bonzo Dog Band playing "By A Waterfall" a cover of a 1933 musical number from the film Footlight Parade, and which, would later appear on the Bonzos' terrific third album "Tadpoles". Splash! Splash! The episode also showcases new member of the team Terry Gilliam and his animated short The Christmas Card, in so doing moving everyone ever closer to that big cut-out foot crashing down on late night BBC One...

---

26 It's a shame that when Channel 4 decided to repeat the episode as part of its Starmaker night (30th December, 1986), Jason apparently demanded to be removed from the edit. Considering his only other contribution to the Christmas of 1986 was the rotten, barely finished "Only Fools and Horses" episode "A Royal Flush" you'd think he'd want a bit of a palette cleanser to hand...

Thursday, 25ᵗʰ December, 1969

12.30pm: Royal Family (BBC One and Two)

"A special Christmas showing of the historic documentary film by Richard Cawston. This unique picture of a year in the life of the Queen and her family has been acclaimed throughout the world and is already established as a television milestone."

This film, ostensibly to celebrate ol' Prince Charles finally being made Prince of Wales, was originally broadcast in June 1969 on both BBC channels <u>and</u> ITV, offering the rare opportunity for a documentary crew to gain access to Buckingham Palace and its environs. It was due to this film that The Queen thought she'd been on TV enough that year and so declined to do an annual Christmas message. If only Mrs Brown's Boys would be equally as considerate.

So with no Liz at 3pm, who was going to replace her...?

3.00pm: With a Little Help from My Friends (ITV)

"George Martin, former recording manager with a top record company and now chairman of his own recording concern, is the man whose knowledge of recording techniques played a great part in the success of the Beatles. Now, for the first time, Martin steps out of the shadows of the pop world for his own show."

Erm...George Martin apparently.

Not the name I'd have naturally assumed as an alternative Queen but, whilst BBC One just bumped up the usual "Billy

Smart's Circus Spectacular" by ten minutes, the light channel finally caught up with the sixties via this Yorkshire TV-produced special starring some of his collaborators including The Hollies, Lulu and Blue Mink plus a nod to his earlier comedy production work on Beyond the Fringe and Bridge on the River Wye among others with Dudley Moore and Spike Milligan. And on hand to run through "Octopus' Garden" was the most available Beatle, Ringo. Not that ITV had gone completely beat groove crazy as many regions shoved a film in this slot whilst Yorkshire who made the damn thing had actually shown it the day before at 6pm.

Friday, 25th December, 1970

12.35pm: The Story of the Silver Skates (BBC One)

"Spectacular skating scenes, including a race-for-life along Holland's frozen canals, are featured in this story about young Hans who tries to help his ailing father by winning a pair of silver skates."

Despite being far from a childhood classic in the UK, Mary Mapes Dodge's 1865 novel was brought singing and dancing into the modern age with music and lyrics by one Moose Charlap. Just take a moment to enjoy that... and we're back. A quaint, well-filmed but tedious musical production enlivened in part by the lead character Hans being played by future "Confessions Of A..." buster-toucher and film rogue Robin Askwith with "Dr. Who and the Daleks" film urchin Roberta Tovey as his sister Gretel. The European co-production means a selection of weird over-dubbed voices giving the impression it's going to turn into full bushed softcore Eurogrot any second. Merry all our Christmasses!

8.30pm: On The Buses (ITV)

"Says Stan: "I've heard of Christmas Day in the workhouse, but this year it's Christmas Day in the depot."

Forever a source of bafflement to most modern audiences, "On The Buses" was one of television's biggest comedy hits of all time, despite its stilted dialogue, grotty sets and grotesque man-child "heroes" trying to constantly have sex with women a third of their age. The key maybe relentless consistency as this edition - "Christmas Duty" in which the characters are saddled with the indignity of having to actually work on Christmas Day - became the 18th new episode of the show to air in 1970 and came midway through the fourth series. The following year, despite the release of such classics as "The French Connection", "Harold and Maude", "The Last Picture Show" and "Shaft", it was the first of three "On the Buses" movies which became Britain's top box office film of the year. It's no wonder Blakey hated their butlers.

Wednesday, 25th December, 1974

8.25pm: Evel Knievel (BBC Two)

"David Frost introduces the attempt by the motor-cycle dare-devil Evel Knievel to pilot his sky-cycle across the Snake River Canyon."

8.45pm: Futtock's End (BBC Two)

"A film starring Michael Hordern, Ronnie Barker and Roger Livesey. Rumbustious goings-on at a country house when the owner, General Futtock, invites a mixed bag of guests for the weekend."

How's that for a double bill? First up, 20 minutes of Lance Murdock-wannabe Knievel risking his life in a steam powered rocket on September 8th, 1974, a stunt he succeeded in with only minor scrapes and cuts. He wouldn't be as lucky in his next big event on May 26th, 1975 as he attempted to jump over 120 feet, over 13 single-decker buses in London. The first 12 buses were fine... the 13th less so and the daredevil knocked himself out, breaking his hand and fracturing his pelvis.

David Frost pops up again although this time only as producer of Ronnie Barker's silent 1970 comedy short "Futtocks End". A knock-about tale of an aristocrat and his troublesome guests to stay – listed in the credits with names like "The Twit" and "The Bird" - to stay does have a bit of Barker's trademark "knickers knackers knockers" nature thanks to several scantily clad ladies but is mostly a pleasurable if not especially hilarious comedy. Likewise if you just want to see the taller Ronnie naked except for strategically placed bubbles this is the film for you!

Thursday, 25th December, 1975

7.55pm: Great Big Groovy Horse (BBC Two)

"A rock-musical romp through the legend of The Wooden Horse of Troy in a version specially written for BBC2 by Simone Bloom and Arnold Shaw".

"Oh what a horse / it's a miracle of course...." An impressive cast for a rockin' hands-to-the-sky spirited one-off including Bernard Cribbins as The Storyteller, with former Manfred Mann-man Paul Jones, Patricia Hodge, Julie Covington and even the future Timothy Claypole himself, Michael Staniforth.

The production was adapted for television in part by Paul Ciani who had a history in marshalling kid-friendly musical variety spectaculars having had directed the likes of "Crackerjack" and "Hope and Keen's Crazy House" whilst the music was composed by Jonathan Cohen who was beloved to the under-fives for his work on BBC children's series "Play School" and its more mischievous weekend spin-off "Play Away". Perhaps reflecting this background, a repeat during children's programming hours came two years later anyway on the 21st December 1977 at 4:40pm.

Tuesday, 25th December, 1979

9.45pm: This is Your Life Special (ITV)

Surprising someone with a big red book around Jesus's birthday was not a novel event by 1979. Early editions of the show used the Christmas edition to surprise a member of the public with early picks being a cleaner named Maud Fairman (1956), seamstress Lucy Jane Dobson (1957) chosen because she'd have "been lonely on Christmas Day", retired postman Richard Bancroft (1960) and Isabella Woodford (1961), a former nurse and Matron of a hospital for military officers. When the series was revived after a five year break by ITV however it was celebs all the way with Les Dawson (1970), Larry Grayson (1971), pianist Gladys "Mrs" Mills (1975) and Muhammad Ali as perhaps the series' biggest coup to date in 1978. By contrast, 1979's guest was probably as beloved in the UK as Ali but had noticeably put Joe Frazier on his arse much less often, being better known for his comedy programmes including "Sykes And A...", "The Likes of Sykes", "The Eric Sykes 1990 Show" and "Sykes".

Spoiler: It was Eric Sykes.

Thursday, 25th December, 1980

5.05pm: 3-2-1 Pantomime (ITV)

"Ted Rogers and the 3-2-1 girls – Fiona Curzon, Karen Palmer, Libby Roberts and Alison Temple Savage – ring up the curtain on this special show. Ted lines up the quips and questions for three pairs of contestants to win top prizes in this family quiz game."

A strange miasma of rock hard cryptic clues, pop singers, comedy turns, celebrity cameos, huge prizes and, of course, a giant comedy bin with a face on it, "3-2-1" should absolutely not have been a hit and yet with the warm, cheery presence of Ted Rogers at the helm it all seemed to just flow quite respectably. Based on a Spanish television format[27] and put out as a bit of easy time filler on a Friday night during the summer in 1978, "3-2-1" was an instant hit and the ratings took off almost immediately leading to a ten year stay on TV. Each edition had a loose theme running throughout and here it was "Cinderella", represented between the rounds with a comic performance of the pantomime "starring" Mike Reid in the role It Doesn't Matter Because He Always Does The Same Bleedin' Thing Every Time (Buttons) alongside Ted's fellow ITV game-show hosts Nicholas Parsons and Derek Batey playing the Ugly Sisters and a rapping Bill Maynard as "The Slave of Dusty Bin". Adding to the "star quotient" was obese MP and alleged sex offender Cyril Smith. Still, the couple win the star prize Ford Escort and a merry Christmas is had by all. Especially if you were watching the other side.

---

[27] "Un, Dos, Tres" devised by Ibáñez Serrador as the jolly animated credits reminded viewers every week. In Spain it ran on and off until 2004. They didn't have a bin on it though.

Saturday, 25th December, 1982

11.40am: Raccoons on Ice (BBC One)

"The lake in the Evergreen Forest is a winter paradise. But Cyril Sneer plans to turn the playground into a colossal concrete complex"

I hated The Raccoons. I hated Burt Raccoon, Alan Raccoon and all the other endlessly-singing, moralistic, finger wagging environmental-pal animal jerks that made up Evergreen Forest in a rotten animated series that seemed to be on throughout my entire effing childhood. I genuinely hoped bad guy and property developer Cyril Sneer would win every week and plough the fuzzy gits into the sod. Before it was a series, the characters first appeared in four TV specials made by Canadian station CBC starting with "The Christmas Raccoons" in 1980, with guest appearances by Rita Coolidge and Rupert Holmes. For this follow up, Holmes was out and our very own dance-feeler Leo Sayer was in. *"Run with us"* the theme song went. Preferably straight into traffic.

Sunday, 25th December, 1983

11.20am: The Little Convict (BBC One)

"Jake the Peg presents the story of the convicts who built Australia."

1.05pm: The Glitterball (BBC One)

"When a spaceship crashlands on earth, its 'pilot' — a small silver ball — is befriended by Max and Pete. They find that the alien being has a vast appetite and can signal to its fellows in space."

A double bill of utterly miserable late 70s kids movies for Christmas Day. The former begins with Rolf's signature hit-that-isn't-about-two-boys "Jake the Peg" before he recounts the partly-animated tale about a young British boy sent on a convict ship headed for New South Wales. Kids must have thrilled to the scene where an old man is crushed to death by a tree. Amazingly it failed to recoup its budget at the Australian box office becoming yet another home-grown film ignored by its own people, a tradition which still holds true today.

For a certain generation the words "Children's Film Foundation" is enough to bring them out in the vapours thanks to Children's BBC filling their schedule with the old cinema short films because their budget had run dry. One of the better ones - which isn't really saying much - "The Glitterball" was in the right genre at the right time for 1977 as "Star Wars" brought sci-fi back in demand. Here was a shitter, cheapo version of them space thrills featuring a bleeping ball-bearing and very little actual space or indeed thrills but lots of oddly fascinating footage of streets, shops and kids fashions acting like a historical document of Britain in the late-seventies.

8.25pm: The King of Comedy (Channel 4)

"Rupert Pupkin has dreamed of being the king of America's stand-up comedians. What he is in fact is a nobody. But then Rupert determines to get an audition from TV comic Jerry Langford"

After numerous examples of having to wait years – even decades – for some cinema films to reach terrestrial TV, here's a rare example of a film making it there within a year of release. For those who haven't seen Scorsese's dark comedy, it's a moody film about delusional people pushed to extreme acts… so a perfect choice for Christmas Day!! Robert De Niro nails the sketchy Pupkin, making him neither a total loser nor a psychopath, while a stunning 27-year old Sandra Bernhard is perfect as a celebrity obsessed stalker and Pupkin's closest contact to anything approaching reality. Even the late, grating Jerry Lewis as the target of both their attentions, chat host Langford, is actually bearable. I suspect more people saw it on Channel 4 than did in the cinema here or America where it was famously a box office disaster.

Tuesday, 25th December, 1984

11.05am: The Noel Edmonds Live Live Christmas Breakfast Show (BBC One)

"From the top of British Telecom Tower, Noel presents a live outside broadcast from 625 feet above London."

Noel Edmonds appearing live on Christmas Morning was an event that only happened five times yet still feels like it was always part of the Christmas Days in my youth. With his experience on "Swap Shop" and the "Late Late Breakfast Show" on Saturday nights Noel was already an old hand at helming a technically intricate live broadcast which was fully put to the test here with lots of outside broadcasts including the much missed Mike Smith out in the "hollycopter". The team would raise the stakes for 1985's show which stretched to a behemoth 125 minutes and featured the *"world's first computer draw"* and, as seen on blooper shows for decades, *"the world's first in-flight pop performance"* with the unfortunate Feargal Sharkey unable to hear anything at 2500ft throughout a mimed performance of "You Little Thief" watched by a helpless and bemused Gary Davies and The Krankies. There was also time for link ups to Africa and the launch of new charity called Comic Relief[28]. 1986 brought a change of title to "Christmas Morning with Noel" to distance it from the "Late, Late Breakfast Show" after its instant cancellation after the unfortunate death of a member of the public during rehearsals for a stunt five weeks earlier. In retrospect, it's amazing the special happened at all, no doubt down to the sheer amount of work that would have gone into setting up satellite links around the world including Australia where it was airing live. These efforts resulted in a duet between Cliff Richard and Elton John both on different continents that is as memorable as it sounds. Plus Mike Smith was looking for Santa in Lapland, how can you miss that? The final show from the top of the Tower would happen in 1987 at the slightly earlier time of 9am due to the show going out live in more countries with New Zealand, Singapore and Gibraltar now joining Australia for across the sea family link ups. With each special previous feeling more and more elaborate the final edition in 1988 was something of a let-down as the show was cut back to just over an hour and even worse came from Studio 3 of BBC TV Centre, a location I'd normally be cock-a-hoop for, but isn't quite the same as being 625 feet above London. The following year saw Edmonds switch to the pre-recorded "Noel's Christmas Presents", a safe but much less fun format that nevertheless became a staple of the Christmas Day schedule for the whole of the nineties with a

---

28 This involved a lot of short filmed sketches of comics trying to tell jokes to tough crowds with Rowan Atkinson trying to raise a smile from BBC One Controller Michael Grade, Lenny Henry doing "I'm not saying my wife is..." jokes to his then-wife Dawn French and Rik and Ade in Dangerous Brothers mode trying to entertain *"a deaf Chinese mountain ant in a matchbox"*.

lengthy revival for Sky later on. Regardless of what we've since learned of him being a bit of an oddball, Noel was always a cheery, personable frontman of these shows who seemed to be genuinely enjoying himself and it was great to feel the BBC was this exciting alive 'being' watching over the world, offering company, and setting out its stall as the channel to stick with all day. And Noel? He hadn't quite finished with live television yet as the doors to his Crinkley Bottom prepared to swing open...

6.00pm: Bring Me Sunshine — A Tribute to Eric Morecambe, OBE (ITV)

"Introduced by Ernie Wise from the London Palladium in the presence of patron Prince Philip and guest of honour Mrs Joan Morecambe the stars pay tribute to a much-loved comedian who died earlier this year."

And as one regular face of Christmas Day telly rose, one of its most beloved sons was suddenly absent. Eric Morecambe and Ernie Wise's final years, when they left BBC One for Thames were not great with a unanimous feeling that the duo were past their best. Even so, it's fair to say that few expected Eric to suddenly not be there when Christmas '84 came around. Eric and Ernie had first appearing as part of BBC One's Christmas Day schedule in 1969 with the relatively low key line-up of Frankie Vaughan and Susan Hampshire but, more importantly, it was the first of the their specials involving Eddie Braben as scriptwriter. Braben had begun to characterise the double act in the roles we would come to love - the buffoon and the hopeless playwright. Their shows continued throughout the seventies only taking a break in 1974 and peaking with the record breaking audiences of Christmas Day 1977. The jump over to

ITV[29] the following year may have seemed abrupt for home audiences but the duo had long wanted to get back to making films and the deal made sense when considering that Thames had the subsidiary Euston Films. Sadly, only "Night Train to Murder" – shown after Morecambe's death – was ever made and, equally sadly, it's bloody awful. Eric and Ernie would make six festive shows for the third channel, initially without Braben who was still contracted to the BBC, with the first three in their regular 25th December slot. However this was the era of regional companies serving the London area: Thames during the week and LWT at weekends and with Christmas Day falling at the weekend between 1981 and 1983, Thames' Morecambe and Wise found itself shunted to, respectively, the 23rd, 27th and 26th of December. And so with Eric's death it's good to see that ITV made space on the Christmas Day schedule for this two and a half hour spectacular including many people who'd worked with the duo such as Michael Aspel, John Thaw, Angela Rippon, Michael Parkinson, Benny Hill, "Not Now" Arthur Tolcher and, naturally, Des O'Connor. Infuriatingly, it also found room for eight minutes of bloody Jim Davidson, the antithesis of everything that made Morecambe such a magnificent comic performer. Still that's done with now and hopefully we won't have to deal with old 'Nick Nick' chops again in this book...

Wednesday, 25th December, 1985

1.00pm: Jim Davidson's Top Pop Videos of '85 (ITV)

"The best-selling pop records from Band-Aid to Bowie and Jagger."

---

29 Or rather jump back as Eric and Ern had been stars of ATV's successful *Two of a Kind* throughout most of the sixties.

Oh for- Really? Did Davidson have a secret cache of photos contains ITV executives in the nip with a marrow and some choir boys or something? I hope he does the "Chalky"[30] voice when discussing the African famine and Band Aid!!!! LOL.

Friday, 25th December, 1987

7.25pm: Christmas Night with the Two Ronnies (BBC One)

"Memo to producer: If the Two Ronnies can actually get Charlton Heston to be in their film Pinocchio II: Killer Doll I will eat my hat. Yours, M. Grade."

And so another institution of British Christmas TV wanders into the sunset. Feeling like the ideas had run dry and they were Barker and Corbett were going through the motions, Ronnie Barker's retirement had been carefully planned and the source of much concealment – Corbett had known for 18 months and faithfully kept the secret – thus meaning that this final special wasn't billed as such with Barker even resisting the urge to say *"and its goodbye from me"* at the very end of recording. As for the show itself its much of the same although it's a mostly fun and cheery 50 minutes. Admittedly, there's a "hilarious" sketch about frugal Yorkshiremen I could live without plus a musical number set in the old West (weren't they all?), a Corbett chair monologue and a guest appearance from Elton John. Elton turns up to do "Candle In The Wind" just recorded live in Australia with the Melbourne Symphony Orchestra, and a hit

---

[30] This was Davidson essaying a stereotypical Jamaican accent and so popular he was even signed to record a cover of "White Christmas" using the voice in 1980. It peaked at No.52.

for the second and presumably final time. But really it's all building up to that final 17 minute "Pinocchio II: Killer Doll" sketch — a horror movie sequel to the Disney classic when Gepetto makes a second wooden boy from an evil tree sprite. The look of the sketch is perfect from costumes to set dressing, the music cues could come from any British video horror nasty of the era, the guest cast are superb and, amazingly, does actually feature Charlton Heston in a brief cameo. The problem is it all actually works TOO well and, despite the gags, it is truly unsettling at times with the scratchy dark old film taking viewers a million miles away from the bright studio lights in the rest of the episode. The sketch ends with a demonic Corbett laughing hysterically as Gepetto burns to death. Merry Christmas everybody! Miss Marple's up next! Oh and Ron's retiring by the way. Tra! The twosome would return one last time to the 25th, sadly after Barker's death, in 2005's best of "The Two Ronnies' Christmas Sketchbook" which wisely left out "Pinocchio II" in favour of some less stool loosening festive fare from their extensive back catalogue.

Sunday, 25th December, 1988

5.30am: Christmas Comes to Pacland (ITV)

In this appalling yet strangely hypnotic special, originally made by Hanna-Barbera in 1982 — just before the US video game market went bang[31] — Pac-Man, Ms. Pac-Man, Pac-Baby,

---

31 This is nothing to do with the abysmal Pac-Man Christmas Album on Kids Stuff Records, also from 1982, in which high pitched voices sing a mixture of copyright free tunes. But not "Pac-Man Fever" by Buckner and Garcia because that would cost money.

Chomp Chomp the Dog and Sour-Puss the Cat help Santa Claus after he crashes on Pac-Land due to his reindeer becoming startled by the floating eyes of the Ghost Monsters munched early in the episode. It's awful but with a naivety that makes it somehow much more bearable and a low-rent heart-warming tale for all...unless you're a ghost. Nobody likes you when you're dead.

1.15pm: The Great British Pop Machine (ITV)

"French and Saunders celebrate the booming success of British pop including Rick Astley, Bros, Erasure, Eurythmics and Kim Wilde."

Phew! Jim Davidson has been sent packing and it's the turn of Dawn and Jennifer, one of the great double acts who mock trendy teen show presenting styles whilst linking performances by the big turns of '88 which, looking back, wasn't much of a halcyon year for pop. The top 10 best sellers of the year featured three covers of 1960s songs (courtesy of Wet Wet Wet, Tiffany and Phil Collins) and one outright re-released song from 1969 (The Hollies' "He Ain't Heavy, He's My Brother".) Thank Baby Jesus that somebody invented the Pet Shop Boys...

Tuesday, 25th December, 1990

5.10pm: Only Fools and Horses (BBC One)

If, as already discussed, The Two Ronnies gave us the scariest Christmas Day telly in 1987, three years on John Sullivan offered us possibly the most depressing in "Rodney Come Home" a genuinely at times bleak 75 minute exploration of

Rodney's failing marriage. Thankfully for viewers fearfully wondering what would happen next, a new series started just five days later on 30th December continuing the soap-plot comedy drama style the programme had edging towards for a few years. Elsewhere on One that same day were festive episodes of "Bread" and "Birds of a Feather" along with the regular chuckle-fest "EastEnders" which all taken together led to potentially one of the most miserable Christmas Day schedules of all time. We should only be grateful "Schindler's List" hadn't been made yet I suppose...

Wednesday, 25th December, 1991

6.00pm: Batman (BBC One)

"First showing on network television of the hit movie starring Michael Keaton and a legend is born."

A stunningly dark film for all the family at tinsel-topped tea time (body count: 56), "Batman" is the movie that ushered in the 12 certificate for cinemas here in Britain and really takes that to the limit. Being nine at the time of its release in 1989 I can remember being geed up to bursting point thanks to all the merchandising – much of it aimed at kids – including Prince's soundtrack but had to wait until an irresponsible cousin let me watch it on video the year after. When it came to the terrestrial TV premiere, it was just as big a deal for BBC One too who even made a special variant on its then-current globe logo which thrillingly became lit up by a giant bat signal. Sadly it didn't get much more use as ITV snapped up the rights to show all the sequels from "Batman Returns" onwards although in the case of 1997's "Batman and Robin" its perhaps no real loss, eh?

Friday, 25th December, 1992

9.00pm: Victoria Wood's All Day Breakfast (BBC One)

"The latest daytime show to be hosted by a popular husband-and-wife team. There are tips on female problems like seriously split ends…"

There were a lot of jokes made at the expensive of ITV's weekday magazine show "This Morning" fronted by married couple Richard Madeley and Judy Finnegan since it launched to huge acclaim in 1988, thanks to its rollercoaster mix of light and heavy topics for discussion, but few were as affectionate yet devastating as Victoria Wood's assassination of the daytime magazine format. Fronted by partners Martin Cumbernauld (Duncan Preston) and Sally Crossthwaite (Wood herself), we find Sally in charge and Martin "with no embarrassment at all" discussing "female problems" like "wonky wombs and faulty fallopian tubes". Between the links are several unconnected sketches including regular visits to "The Mall" which did for the BBCs new soap flop "Eldorado" what Wood's earlier "Acorn Antiques" had for Crossroads with its light inconsequential plots and wooden acting. There's also a predictable but fun connection to Wood's earlier work in the final part. The special ends with some new stand-up and new song "Real Life" *("Life is a fan club and I'm not a fan / Life is a bran tub / no prizes / just bran"*), later to become the title track of her only studio album in 1997. It's tempting, watching Wood interview – slash - insult old friend and special guest Alan "'Dickman'" Rickman, to and not feel a bit melancholy at the fact both are no longer with us but when the comedy is this good we'll always be laughing too much to allow that.

December 26th

BARRRRRRRRRPPPP...Oh lord, I feel like I've swallowed an armchair, my left leg is currently on strike and the inside of my mouth tastes like a thousand parties I wish I hadn't been invited to. Yep, it must be Boxing Day! Or, in my house as it's also my mum's birthday, Christ-Did-I-Remember-To-Buy-Two-Giftsmas Day.

For many Boxing Day translates to "SALES!" and even in the digital age you can guarantee, some loons have been camped outside Next or Ians The Shoe since 4am to fight with some old biffer over a pair of 30% off stretched denim waders you wouldn't normally be seen dead in. For me, the modern Boxing Day is probably best spent finally getting a quiet moment to yourself to watch all the programmes from Christmas Day that your relatives talked over. How will you ever know if Mrs Brown fell over and said "feck" when your Auntie Chris is banging on about her rupture? Did they call the midwife yet? Which one is Shrek 2? And did Strictly come whilst dancing again?

Boxing Day on TV tends to be the refuge of the Not Ready For Prime Time shows that wouldn't necessarily bring in the punters on their own but are always worth the wait. For example, "Outnumbered" is one of the great sitcoms of the last decade but it's a bit too dry to be appreciated after a whole roast chicken and eight glasses of fizz. Christmas Day is for the broad and simple, Boxing Day is for the soul. Or, at the very least, it's for the second box of Celebrations you've got stashed behind the settee.

Mum happy with her Cliff Richard calendar and charcoal briquettes from the garage? Excellent, let's watch us some TV...

9.00pm: Not Only.... But Also (BBC Two)

"In this traditional season of goodwill the minds of Peter Cook and Dudley Moore have followed their natural bent..."

The first of a number of Peter Cook recurrences in this chapter, this 1966 special had him in a number of guises including Hiram J Pipesucker, host of Idaho's "Pipesucker Report", which looked at "swinging London". Making a guest appearance was John Lennon[32] as the doorman to the hottest private members club in town the 'Ad Lav'[33] which also happened to be a public convenience. The real highlight of the episode also had a touch of The Beatles about it with the affectionate but brutal pastiche of psychedelic pop "The L.S Bumblebee". Despite the rather un-Fabs sounding cries of *"Oh druggy druggy!"* and *"freak out baby, the bee is coming!"* – not to mention the rather more obvious joke in that it says "bum" a lot – the legend goes that less clued up or perhaps simply mischievous US DJs picked up on the song and played it as a track from the new Beatles LP which was bootlegged accordingly for years. Unlike many sixties music parodies you can see why people might have been fooled due to its gorgeous production and genuinely catchy tune[34]. Equally, those crazy Beatles were known for liking a laugh and John Lennon had just appeared on the Christmas special of a zany British comedy series you know. Now what was it called again...?

---

32 He previously appeared on the NO...BA pilot in January 1965.
33 A spoof of the real-life swinging hotspot the 'Ad Lib' club.
34 It was released as a single by Decca the following January backed with Pete and Dud's anti-drug talk "The Bee Side."

Tuesday, 26th December, 1967

4.35pm: The Sad/Happy Ending Story of the Bald Twit Lion (BBC Two)

"The world première of a story for very all ages."

Another one on the teetering genius front. I have to confess I've never been much of a fan of Milligan's television stuff, preferring his wordplay on the page, so I'm interested in this half-hour this adaptation of one of his children's short stories about a very silly lion called Mr Gronk who roars so loud all his hair falls out and needs God's help to put it back. A picture book version, featuring Carol Barker's gorgeous drawings from the broadcast, was published in 1968 and good quality copies now fetch a substantial amount. Luckily for those with less bulging wallets the story also appeared in the much easier to find "A Book of Milliganimals" accompanied by Milligan's own unique artwork.

8.35pm: The Beatles (BBC One)

"Present their own film Magical Mystery Tour with songs & music."

Or The Beatles fanny about for two weeks in September in a bus full of their mates and funny people with no real script having an amazing time and occasionally singing some new songs. And what's wrong with that? Especially when "Magical Mystery Tour"'s songs are as good as "Your Mother Should Know", "The Fool on the Hill" and the title track itself, all of which had been made available a few weeks earlier on a double EP release for fans to learn off by heart. All this plus bonus

Bonzo Dog Band and poet Ivor Cutler too. Broadcast in black and white with a second showing in colour on BBC Two on 5th January 1968 the film was hated by critics due to its meandering nature and wouldn't get another repeat until Two's The Beatles at Christmas season in 1979.

Saturday, 26th December, 1970

1.30pm: Cucumber Castle (BBC Two)

"A medieval musical starring The Bee Gees with Eleanor Bron, Pat Coombs and special guest stars Blind Faith, Frankie Howerd, Lulu, Spike Milligan and Vincent Price"

Spike Milligan's back again as court jester to a castle full of people who don't seem to quite know what's going on as The Bee Gees, now down to just Barry and Maurice, try their own version of "Magical Mystery Tour" with much less convincing results. It featured their recent number 2 hit "Don't Forget to Remember" – which ironically most people have now forgotten - along with four other songs from their already flopped album which had been released in April 1970, but had stalled at number 57 in the UK charts. In fact "Cucumber Castle" marked the Gibb's last charting LP until John Travolta's swaying crotch propelled them back into the limelight in 1978. The film feels like wading through treacle at times when compared to The Beatles' earlier extravaganza and whilst it's nice to see the likes of Frankie Howerd, Vincent Price and Pat Coombs doing their usual schtick as The Gibbs attempt to keep up, it does feel like something Peter Cook and Dudley Moore might have knocked together in a particularly lazy afternoon. Speaking of which...

6.45pm: Holiday Startime (ITV)

"A galaxy of top comedy stars and top musical performers with Ted Ray, Arthur Lowe, Thora Hird, Peter Cook and Les Dawson."

...here is Cook at a strange time in his career which was still big but hadn't really rocketed like many had expected; the third and final series of "Not Only...But Also" over that year and his performance in fun media satire "The Rise and Rise of Michael Rimmer" slated by critics. Returning to the character E.L Wisty, the park bench philosopher and bore with whom he'd become famous through appearances via ITV's "On the Braden Beat" in the early sixties, must have felt like retreating to the safety of old overcoat. "Holiday Startime" was an incredibly MOR show featuring mostly standard comics and music from...oh it's only the bloody Bee Gees again! Thankfully for Cook the hit stage show "Behind the Fridge" was around the corner along with the creation of a distinctly non-TV friendly duo Derek and Clive. How interesting.

8.30pm: 'Wilton's': The Handsomest Hall in Town (BBC Two)

"Tonight, 90 years after it closed, this famous Music-Hall opens again to bring you a picture of the stars, the singers, the dancers, and the people who once went there."

An all-star tribute to the days of music hall very much in the style of BBC One's "The Good Old Days" and written by old timey enthusiast Jimmy Perry, best known at that point for co-creating "Dad's Army". Part of the reason this one-off managed to get such a great cast – Peter Sellers, Spike Milligan, Warren

Mitchell and Ronnie Barker – can be traced to Wilton's Music Hall itself, a real life East End London locale active between 1859 and 1888, and the special doffed its extremely tall hat to with a recreation of the sort of show that would have been seen at the time. Many of the performers waived their fees in order for the money to go towards the refurbishment of the building with Sellers and Milligan just two of the celebrity supporters of the site after it was announced that the building was to be knocked down in the late sixties. The movement worked and the site was given Grade II listed building status in April 1971, just four months after this broadcast. Since then much restoration work has taken place and the venue is once again used for shows. Perry's continued love of performing directly influenced his next major sitcom project with David Croft about a touring concert party in the Second World War called "It Ain't Half Hot Mum". It is rubbish. More interesting was "Turns" a meticulously researched documentary series he hosted for the BBC between 1982 and 1989 on variety acts of the pre-WWII era.

Sunday, 26th December, 1971

6.00pm: Opportunity Knocks! (ITV)

"Welcome to the Opportunity Knocks! Variety Club Special, when the top artist receives the coveted Variety Club award. A number of the Club's stars have promised to attend on this gala occasion, including Saint cum Persuader, Roger Moore."

I'm sure I remember seeing "Saint Cum Persuader" written on a tape my mate's dad kept in his sock drawer. This was the year of "Wee" Neil Reid, a "darling" 12 year old Scottish boy who went to number two in the charts with the sensitive, emotional and, above all, rotten ballad "Mother Of Mine" which was only kept off the top spot by The New Seekers insisting on teaching the world to sing. His album, however, went one place better and was number one for three weeks knocking T-Rex's "Electric Warrior" off the perch before being usurped by Neil Young's "Harvest". Reid's second single stalled at 41 and he sensibly gave up show-business when his bollocks dropped.

Wednesday, 26th December, 1973

4.30pm: H.M.S. Pinafore (ITV)

"Gilbert's witty class satire with Sullivan's glittering music performed by the D'Oyly Carte Opera Company."

Blimey! Gilbert and Sullivan performed on ITV in the "Tipping Point" slot! What next? "The Flintstones" on ice!?

Friday, 26th December, 1975

1.00pm: The Flintstones on Ice (ITV)

"From the Stone Age to the Ice Age. The Flintstones show amazing grace when they put themselves on ice in a skate spectacular."

...WHAT?!? A CBS production for Christmas 1973, this had animated wraparounds featuring the original voice cast of "The Flintstones" but it was a long way from their respected prime-time sitcom of the early sixties. By 1971, the modern stone age family had moved to Saturday mornings with "The Pebbles and

Bamm-Bamm Show", a spin-off featuring the teenage children of Fred and Barney who naturally had their own rock band (The Bedrock Rockers), before "The Flintstone Comedy Hour" took its place with those ghastly fake laugh tracks that seemed ridiculous in an animated programme. Especially one that wasn't very funny like this.

10.55pm: Christmas with Rutland Weekend Television (BBC Two)

"From Britain's tiniest TV network – an evening of mini-spectacular programmes with Rutland's own favourite stars including Eric Idle, Neil Innes and singing guest artist George Harrison."

Let loose after the dissolution of the "Flying Circus" all the Pythons seemed to have a fantastic solo project up and running before the end of the seventies – be it "Fawlty Towers", "Ripping Yarns", "Jabberwocky" or not dying of alcohol poisoning. "Rutland Weekend Television" was Eric Idle's baby and purported to be the line-up of Britain's smallest independent TV station. Made on a shoestring budget, the cheap and cheerful nature of the premise was also somewhat of a necessity although Idle had a deep enough address book to ensure some excellent support from ex-Bonzo Dog man Neil Innes and, for this episode only, George Harrison of "The Concert For Bangladesh" fame. Naturally there's a caveat and it's that Harrison wants to perform in a pirate sketch against the wishes of Idle. Elsewhere, there's a lesson on How To Ski In Your Own Home, film of HM Queen of Rutland's right royal year, Innes performing "I Don't Believe in Santa Any More" and the centrepiece of the show "Rutland Film Night" with a savage but slyly appreciative look at a familiar looking new rock musical "Pommy" ("He'll tear your ears apart") featuring another Innes original, "Concrete Jungle Boy", a Who pastiche as good as anything in The Who's real film. As we'll see shortly, rock musicals were the big thing in the mid-seventies and *RWT* nails them thoroughly in just five minutes. The show ends with the return of George Harrison, free of his earlier pirate costume, to sing his number one hit "My Sweet Lord". Or does he...? Never released on DVD and rarely rebroadcast[35], Idle would later annoy his remaining fans when he announced on Twitter that the series was returning for Christmas 2016. Instead we got the grim Brian-Cox-show-pastiche-but-with-Brian-Cox-in-it spoof "The Entire Universe".

Sunday, 26th December, 1976

6.25pm: Rock Nativity (ITV)

"Rock Nativity is a stage musical about the birth of Christ, which has been adapted as a studio presentation for television."

Monday, 26th December, 1977

1.45pm: Orion (BBC Two)

"The world is coming to an end and the last survivors board a spaceship ready to leave the doomed Earth in search of a new world."

See? Rock musicals as far as the eye can wossname! The former

---

35 See the later entry for "At Home with Vic and Bob".

of these two rockstravangazas is unsurprisingly a telling of the Jesus boy birth tied to the power of ROCK! Music was supplied by former husband and wife team Tony Hatch and Jackie Trent (whose ridiculously catchy theme to "Neighbours" sound-tracked dining tables for decades.) "Rock Nativity" was a rare nationwide production for Scottish network STV and captured the musical after a nationwide tour. Writer of the book and lyrics for the show David Wood described the musical on his website[36] as the *"modern equivalent of the medieval mystery play – simple yet not naïve, humorous yet not disrespectful, devotional yet not overtly pious"*. Having watched a later presentation made for Irish station RTE on YouTube I would add the word "boring" and question the use of the word "rock" in the title. Still its better than "Highway" I suppose.

"Orion" on the other hand was a sci-fi "Noah's Ark in Space" with a book by none other than the Sinex-sniffing supremo himself Melvyn Bragg. A soundtrack was never released but it's a fair bet that it's an adaptation of 1969's "Ark 2", the only studio album by Flaming Youth, featuring songs written by Ken Howard and Alan Blaikley better known at the time for writing more conventional pop hits. On drums was a pre-Genesis joining teenager called Phil Collins who writes about the experience in his autobiography Not Dead Yet: *"Ark 2 is unveiled with a publicity stunt launch at London's Planetarium. By now I'm squirming at all this ultra-fab cod-psychedelia; it's both pretentious and cartoonish."* Howard and Blaikley would go on to write several other musicals including an adaptation of "The Secret Diary of Adrian Mole" for the West End.[37]

---

36 http://www.davidwood.org.uk/plays/plays_rock_navity.htm
37 You can hear samples via www.kenhoward-alanblaikley.com

Sunday, 26th December, 1982

3.30pm: The Krankies Christmas Club (ITV)

"Christmas at the Krankies' Community Centre ..."

Krankies...Community Centre? Its council spending gone mad! An acquired taste, those two Krankies, unquestionably a well-rehearsed act that Ian and Jeanette Tough have worked on for decades but it's just a bit wearing after a few minutes. Initially breaking through via the long-running "Crackerjack" the Toughs next moved to LWT for the early-Saturday evening "The Krankies Klub" which began with this 1982 Christmas special. They were later one of the few acts, along with Roland Rat and Russ Abbot, to head to the BBC in the mid-eighties when everyone else was going the other way, where they occupied much the same timeslot and show – now called "The Krankies Elektronik Komik". It's actually his wife you know!

6.15pm: The Snowman (Channel 4)

"An animated version, produced to appeal to audiences of all ages, of the well-known children's story."

And so a legend begins, initially with author Raymond Briggs introducing the tale as the higher profile David Bowie opening was only added in 1983, the animation of Briggs' 1978 book is still stunning all these years on and it's still being shown on Channel 4 long after the rest of the station went rubbish. Even more exciting than any of that was Quicksilva's 1984 Spectrum version of the story where the young boy has to avoid various monsters in order to build up his titular frozen friend with game-play reminiscent of the much more successful "Jetpac". Upon completing each level the game would play a bleepy version of that classic song associated with "The Snowman" – that's right – "Rudolph The Red Nosed Reindeer". No wonder he couldn't wait to melt...

Friday, 26th December, 1986

10.00pm: Max Headroom's Giant Christmas Turkey (Channel 4)

"Live and direct from Max's own fireside – and Max knows you just won't be able to resist this huge fat bird."

Th-th-there are few faces that accurately convey the eighties as a decade more than a stuttering Matt Frewer covered in latex. Max was one of those rare transatlantic hits who seemed, almost overnight, to be everywhere from chat shows to adverts. There was also his terrific "20 Minutes into the Future" TV movie and its well-received but short-lived action drama spin-off for ABC which opened up the creation of Max and pitched his world in a cyberpunk future. This 1986 special though, is closer to his regular format of pop videos and interviews, although the former have been jettisoned in favour of new Max-crooned numbers backed by The Southwark Cathedral Choir. Plus interviews with Tina Turner, Robin Williams and Bob Geldof who Max persuades into "writing" a song – "Merry Christmas Santa Claus (You're A Lovely Guy)" - which had genuinely been released as a single earlier that year but sadly for Max fl-fl-flopped. Frickin' liberal.

1.05pm: Saint And Greavsie's Boxing Day Special (ITV)

"Festive fun and frolics from Ian St John and Jimmy Greaves as they preview the all-important Boxing Day programme and spring a few surprises."

Football's a winner and the ref's okay. As if it wasn't boring enough, Boxing Day is for many a day of sport and here's the light-hearted pre-match whimsy of the Ian and Jimmy who weren't The Krankies. "Saint and Greavsie" ran from 1985 until the loss of the Premier League rights to Sky in 1992 and, whilst easily mocked, actually made the game accessible and entertaining to non-fans like myself in the same way Baddiel and Skinner would with "Fantasy Football League" a decade later.[38] Without Saint and Greaves now, who have got? No seriously, I'm asking. I genuinely don't know.

11.55pm: A Bit of Fry and Laurie (BBC One)

"Thirty minutes of exquisitely-tooled comedy, embossed with a personalised monogram of up to two of your favourite initials. Available in Moroccan peach or executive silver."

Can you imagine any channel putting out the pilot for a new comedy sketch series at five to midnight on Boxing Day now? This terrific introduction sets out Stephen and Hugh's already

---

[38] Although that series' savage running sketch "Saint and Greavsie Talk About The Endsleigh League As If Its Im-portant" featuring an endlessly chuckling Ian and a weeping Jim was incredibly funny.

well-honed act admirably to new viewers although the pair already had quite a pedigree: after the Cambridge Footlights had come BBC Two pilot "The Crystal Cube", ITV sketch shows "There's Nothing to Worry About!" and "Alfresco" and weekly spots on Channel 4's explosive variety show "Saturday Live". Sketches in this first edition of their own BBC series introduce many of the themes that would become synonymous with the pair with a gallery of buffoons, bores and bloody! business! men! Highlights include The Privatisation of the Police Force which is then dismantled by duelling arts shows, Hugh's exquisite jazz ballad "Mystery" about an increasingly unlikely romance (*"Taken a violent dislike to me / I'd be foolish to ignore the possibilities / That if we had ever actually met / you might have hated me / Still, that's not the only problem that I can see / Dead since 1973..."*) and a suitably over-the-top parody of convoluted Australian soap opera plots (*"You mean we've been sleeping together all this time...behind my back?"*) Viewers would have to wait until January 1989 for a full series, now screened on BBC Two, although in the interim the double act recorded the magnificent Radio 4 series "Saturday Night Fry" (30th April – 4th June 1988) which in many ways feels like a dry run for the TV series proper.

Monday, 26th December, 1988

7.20pm: Civvy Street (BBC One)

Hugely hyped at the time and strangely forgotten now "Civvy Street" was the first spin off from "EastEnders" at its hip, gritty peak back when its cast all became stars overnight and started to have hit singles alongside all sorts of merchandising. Soon two episodes a week was beginning to seem not enough. Enter

"Civvy Street", set during wartime in 1942 and featuring older characters from the modern series such as Lou Beale, Ethel Skinner and even Reg Cox who was found dead in the very first episode, as youths. Despite a script by the original series' co-creator Tony Holland, the special was only a small success with its audience of seven million viewers lagging some way behind the parent soap's ratings of 21.1 million that same week. It probably didn't help that the same year saw the broadcast of a very similar prequel series "First of the Summer Wine" with the youthful adventures of Clegg, Compo and the other one.

10.55pm: Bruce and Ronnie (BBC One)

"...in the Corbett and Forsyth Show. Still chuckling after their first appearance as a team – at the Royal Variety Performance..."

Despite featuring heavily in the pre-season trailers, this post-Ronnies special featuring the odd pairing of Forsyth and Corbett was buried in a strangely terrible timeslot by the schedulers. It's a pity as, despite looking a bit dated by 1988 standards with its dancing girls and shiny floor presentation[39], it's not a bad one-off at all with the two leads are in good form choosing to play their new union akin to squabbling brothers poking light fun at each other's careers. Both get their own solo spot too, with Forsyth playing a jazz number and Corbett, naturally, doing a chair monologue. The programme ends with a "Gone with the Wind" sketch that feels more like a Morecambe and Wise sketch minus the wise. No more were commissioned and now they're both dead. THANKS FOR NOTHING BBC.

---

[39] It was also broadcast immediately after the much hipper "The Lenny Henry Special" which can't have helped.

Wednesday, 26th December, 1990

9.50pm: A Life in Pieces (BBC Two)

"Sir Arthur Streeb-Greebling chooses his 12 Christmas gifts in conversation with Ludovic Kennedy."

And we're back to Peter Cook who returned to another old character – the multi-purpose aristocrat, failed restaurateur and bore Streeb-Greebling – to record a dozen five minute pieces vaguely connected to the 12 days of Christmas. Not his career best but it was good to see Cook on TV being funny in a late resurgence that would happily soon be capitalised upon with memorable appearances on "Have I Got News for You", "Clive Anderson Talks Back" and (back in the guise of Sir Arthur) for an obscure but wonderful Radio 3 series called "Why Bother?" which used the comic in a way rarely heard before in part due to his young, aggressive inquisitor and collaborator Chris Morris.

Sunday, 26th December, 1993

9.05pm: One Foot in the Algarve (BBC One)

"The only place to seek holiday accommodation in Portugal is to trawl through the classified ads in Zit magazine – at least that's irascible Victor Meldrew's method in this special feature length story."

And for the final time, here's Cook again in sadly the worst episode of *One Foot in the Grave* as a shady photographer brilliantly named Martin Trout who the Meldrews encounter over a mix up regarding a saucy roll of film on their feature-length holiday break. Seen by a remarkable series best audience of 20 million, it isn't terrible except when judged against the rest of its own brilliance. Writer David Renwick was quoted on the subject of not making it seem padded out like most sitcom films: *"I ended up going the other way, packing the script with too many ideas and story lines and it became indigestible."* Terrible weather and Cook's general lack of real desire to learn his lines word perfectly also affected the filming although many of the improvised replacement pieces Peter came up with stayed in the torturous final edit due to their quality. A year later, the show's fifth series began on Christmas Day itself, for "The Man Who Blew Away" now safely back on home turf and only slightly extended to forty minutes. It's also one of the bleakest episodes of anything ever to be shown on the big day – editions of "Mrs Brown's Boys" not permitting...

December 27th

December 27th

What? Is it still Christmas? I hate Christmas. Christmas is the worst. To protest I'm going to sit here and watch "Shrek Goes To The Moon" in my pants and burrow through enough Guylian chocolates to stun a large weasel.

I remember watching of all things "The Movie Game Christmas Special" one year, as hosted by future bum-baring menace John Barrowman, when my friend Marc turned to me and said *"Christmas specials after Christmas are just depressing, aren't they?"* A very true thought that has never left me to this day. These shows were clearly recorded nowhere near the festive period, months before with a team of people faking it as best they can, only to be scheduled on December 27th when everyone's cracker hats have torn and the last thing anyone wants to see is a well-paid TV host wishing them a Merry Christmas from back in August when it all still seemed like a good idea.

It's not necessarily down to the quality of the programmes, though, as we'll discover, merely how popular certain franchises are in a now much bigger television playground. "Call the Midwife"? Go straight to Christmas Day, girlfriend. "Text The Gynaecologist"? Erm...just stay away from my turkey, please.

Of course it could be really bad and you have to go work. Maybe some more "Shrek" and chocolates might not be such a terrible thing after all...

Saturday, 27ᵗʰ December, 1969

10.15pm: A Child of the Sixties (ITV)

"A whole generation has grown up which simply does not know what life without television could possibly have been like. A Child of the Sixties will examine this last decade through the eyes of a young man whose knowledge and understanding of the world around him was shaped, almost exclusively, by television."

And that child's name was...Gyles Brandreth. No, really it was!

"Gyles Brandreth in his last year at Oxford was 11 in 1960. He is an Oxford undergraduate, President of the Union, co-editor of Isis[40] and directed the Oxford University Dramatic Society." (TV Times)

Known by most as either that gaudily jumpered git on "TV-am" or the old posh chap who never stops talking on "The One Show", Brandreth has lived a fascinating life and his genuinely fascinating collection of diaries "Something Sensational To Read On The Train" bears out some of the incredible things he was involved with including this special which was taped on 15ᵗʰ December 1969 at the London Weekend studios with guests historian Lady Longford, TV producer and former president of CBS News Fred Friendly and the MPs Iain Macleod and Michael Foot of Conservative and Labour respectively. After the broadcast, the Daily Sketch suggested of Brandreth *"a new Frost is born"* whilst another newspaper headline described him as the *"heart-throb of the seventies"*. They never saw the jumpers coming...

---

40 Not that one.

Sunday, 27th December, 1972

3.05pm: Dr Who and the Sea Devils (BBC One)

"Now you can see again the whole of the Doctor's struggle against the Master & the strange creatures from the bottom of the sea."

Originally screened as six parts between February and April 1972, whoever decided to put together these omnibus editions of Malcolm Hulke's Who serial together is one of those geniuses like Einstein or the other bloke with the face. Not only is it perfect filler for a boring day but it also brought the Third Doctor tale to a bigger audience (8.7 million) who may have avoided the programme as merely a kids show. As we all know it is a very serious science fiction series and no more so when The Doctor's adversary for this episode The Master, played perfectly with a mixture of smarts and sarcasm by Roger Delgado, sits in his prison cell during one scene happily watching "The Clangers" and becoming enraptured by the *"extraterrestrial life forms"* before being disappointed to learn they're just puppets. And his full name is Dr. Who cos that's what it says in the *Radio Times* so there.

Monday, 27th December, 1976

11.15am: Swap of the Pops (BBC One)

"Noel Edmonds invites you to a SOLID SILVER SWAP with Keith Chegwin and Abba at a Multi-Coloured Boxing Day gig."

Combining two Edmonds projects into a Super Mecha Noelosaurus, "Multi-Coloured Swap Shop" had only started in

October 1976 and took off quickly, setting the format for pretty much every Saturday morning magazine show that followed, with a mix of phone-ins, star guests, cartoons and competitions. "Swap of The Pops" was the regular pop music slot on the show and acts would also bring on unique prizes to win. It's often said that rough kids watched "TISWAS" whilst poshos watched "Swap Shop" but maybe it's just that some children weren't as into watching the cast of "The Comedians" throw foam at young women. The line-up for this first special was the best musical guests over the show's autumn run, with Mud, Showaddywaddy, Pussycat, The Wurzels and Dr Hook all of whom are probably on the same bill as each other at a festival in Great Yarmouth right now. Later on BBC One that day were even more tunes in "Parkinson's Music" (11.05pm) featuring highlights of TV's miserable old bastard asking Fred Astaire, Sammy Davis Jr, Duke Ellington, Dudley Moore, Elton John, Oscar Peterson, Buddy Rich and Andy Williams when Jamie Cullum was due to be born. *"If ye didnae have ye wellies..."*

Sunday, 27th December, 1977

7.55pm: The Little and Largest Show on Earth (BBC One)

"Syd Little and Eddie Large invite you to join them and their guests under the Big Top at Belle Vue, Manchester."

Another act who first broke through on the popular TV talent show "Opportunity Knocks" which led to a series for Thames in early 1977 called *"The Little And Large Tellyshow"*[41] before

---

41 The one episode of Tellyshow I've seen would make me take up Ebola-gargling as a career ahead of watching it again.

the BBC swooped in for what would eventually be a 14-year stretch with the Corporation. As someone who loves light entertainment and good comedy I can safely say I never got the appeal of these two at all with their act seemingly consisted of Large interrupting and mocking Little, all the while looking like they couldn't actually stand the other. Collectors of fine vinyl might wish to know that an LP from the same year – "Soopersonic Syd Sings (Or Does He?)" – now goes for very nearly £3.74 on music site Discogs.

Thursday, 27th December, 1979

11.10pm: Richard Stilgoe (BBC Two)

"Stilgoe takes a break from the news of the week to reflect on some of the stories of the year and look optimistically into the 80s."

Richard Stillnotdead[42] was the face of gentle satirical tunes on any TV show who fancied one in the 1970s and 80s. Stilgoe's own teatime BBC Two series And Now the Good News... started in October 1978 with a remit of presenting *"an optimists' guide to the news of the week"* before moving to a late evening slot in a show under his own name. Many true Stilgovians believe his peak was during the coverage of Election 79 when he broke up the misery of Maggie's first victory with a genuinely hypnotic musical recap of many of the night's results. Often derided for being twee his songs revelled in wordplay and topicality with a lot more bite than memory recalls and Stilgoe perhaps deserves a bit of a late career reappraisal.

---

42 As the *Mary Whitehouse Experience* cruelly dubbed him.

Saturday, 27th December, 1980

5.20pm: A Cup O' Tea an' a Slice O' Cake (ITV)

"All-singing, all-dancing Worzel Gummidge special which examines the important role that scarecrows play in helping Santa Claus..."

Nothing terrified me as a child like Worzel Gummidge. My two-year-old self didn't care that co-writers Keith Waterhouse and Willis Hall were local Leeds lads behind projects like "Whistle Down the Wind", "Budgie" or "Billy Liar". Likewise Jon Pertwee wasn't yet the singing, dancing Third Doctor to me. He was a scary, grubby bugger who spends the first two minutes of this particular special vindicating my terror by standing at a family's window and gawping in. Can you imagine turning round and finding the scarecrow from up in the field stood looking at you with a dopey grin on its face? You'd feel certain he wanted to swallow your soul. Elsewhere, special guest stars Bill Maynard, Billy Connolly and Barbara Windsor (as "Saucy Nancy") turn up to sing a few numbers. Which, naturally, means they're all dead to me now.

Sunday, 27th December, 1981

7.15pm: The Goodies Christmas Special (ITV)

"Just when you thought it was safe to go back to the pantomime..."

Having waited a year for the visual effects department at the BBC to not be needed on "The Hitchhikers Guide to the Galaxy" or "Doctor Who", Bill Oddie, Graeme Garden and Tim Brooke-Taylor decided to leave the BBC after a decade and finally take up ITV on one of their regular offers to defect to their side. Until the release of a DVD collecting these episodes in 2007, it had been received wisdom they weren't very good. In fact, it turns out to be their strongest run in years, with only this spoof of everything from video nasties to pantomime cows being slightly weak. In "Snow White 2", the Superchaps Three join the seven dwarves as *"Soppy, Grotty and...Tim"* before fighting for sexual equality in the female-led world of panto roles. Needing dwarves in a UK production it's no surprise to see Rusty Goffe, David Rappaport, Mike Edmonds, Jack Purvis and Kenny Baker in the cast list all of whom were hot from appearing in that year's magnificent "Time Bandits".

.

Monday, 27th December, 1982

8.05pm: The Funny Side of Christmas (BBC One)

"A specially written show taking a lighthearted view of the festive season. Introduced by Frank Muir."

A selection box of sketches and new scenes from the most popular comedy series on both channels, including "The Fall and Rise of Reginald Perrin", "Yes Minister", "Three of a Kind" and new kid on the block "Only Fools and Horses" – from which the eight minute "Christmas Trees" has become one of the series' most desperately sought after items. There's also Les Dawson and Roy Barraclough as Cissie and Ada and a great hospital sketch by Mel Smith and Griff Rhys Jones – which feels a little like an audition skit as "Not the Nine O'Clock News" had finished in March 1982 and the duo were still a year away from their own series "Alas Smith and Jones". Bizarrely the whole special was repeated again at the height of summer on Monday 22nd August 1983.

Tuesday, 27th December, 1983

8.50pm: Last of the Summer Wine (BBC One)

"Compo, Clegg and Foggy reluctantly sneak Sam out of his invalid bed for a final frolic with the not so young as she used to be Lily-Bless-Her. Then drops them right in it by becoming far more trouble dead than alive..."

I'm not sure when the critical consensus on "Last of the Summer Wine" turned from changed from affection and admiration to sneery dismissal. Perhaps it was Vic and Bob's admittedly funny if a little unfair "Three Blokes In A Bath" spoof in a much played BBC advert during the mid-nineties, or perhaps because it went on for 31 series and was stuck in an increasingly earlier Sunday teatime slot for the last twenty or so series. There was a lot more depth than bathtubs and ogling elderly women going on, though, and Roy Clarke's writing deserves more praise than it gets for the way it told character-driven stories and, in the case of this special "Getting Sam Home", writing a feature-length episode for TV long before John Sullivan made it popular. Shot entirely on film and presented without a laugh track, the story was based on Clarke's own 1974 novel – simply titled "Last of the Summer Wine" – which featured the original trio Clegg, Compo and Blamire, played by Michael Bates in the first two series and replaced here by Brian Wilde's Foggy. Guest star Lynda Baron plays a rare female in the series that actually seems to enjoy sex but still with an underlying sadness. There's a touch of the "Weekend at Bernie'"s in there and some daft slapstick but it's a genuinely beautiful film about death, sex and the passing of time that might just surprise people who only saw the latter episodes, particularly after Bill Owen's passing.

Friday, 27th December, 1985

7.30pm: A Tube Special Report: "And Tonight Thank God It's Them Instead of You" (Channel 4)

"This programme looks at the making of Do They Know It's Christmas?, goes backstage at Wembley during Live Aid and reports on the progress made to combat famine in Ethiopia and the Sudan."

And it won't be snowing Africans this Christmas time. Despite the best attempts of Roland Rat the biggest thing of 1985 was undoubtedly "Live Aid" which was watched by an estimated global audience 1.9 billion across 150 nations....and it still didn't get a series!!! Stolen Harry Hill jokes aside, however you feel about charity concerts like this, there really never will be an event to compare with the scale and reach which is even more impressive when the tales of Bob Geldof just announcing people so they had to play in order to not look like arseholes came out years later. And he said *"f**k the address"* if we're doing bad impressions accurately, okay?

Sunday, 27th December, 1987

12.00pm: The Chart Show Christmas Special (Channel 4)

"All those who thought Christmas was over, stand by for this special seasonal edition of The Chart Show, featuring the Top 10 singles of the year and a selection of the best sellers of 1987."

Before it became the dependable bridge between Saturday morning kids shows and Jimmy Greaves' face, "The Chart Show" had been devised to fill the Channel 4 schedule on

Friday tea-times when its flagship pop series "The Tube" was on holiday and made an immediate impact thanks to its impressive video recorder-inspired computer graphics and lack of host. It was also the only place that you could ever hope to see a snippet of your indie, dance or rock favourites in an era long before genre specific music channels.

As it was the end of the year, it meant spurious awards and New Order's "True Faith" grabbed best video of the year whilst "Talking Of Love" — Anita Dobson's totally forgotten follow up to "Anyone Can Fall In ~~Custard~~ Love" — was dubbed Worst. Best New Act was the still quite fashionable Wet Wet Wet whose first two albums are indelibly stamped on my brain thanks to my Dad's love of them at the time. INXS's "Need You Tonight" was "The One That Got Away" due to its initial No.58 chart placing, whilst their semi-countrymen Crowded House received the starkly titled Best Foreign Video for "Don't Dream Its Over". Better than its successor "CD:UK" and much harder to invade, "The Chart Show" was the pop show with something for everyone. Long live the UK music scene!

10.00pm: A Non-Denominational Spitting Image Holiday Special (ITV)

"An unmistletoeable Christmas cracker of a pudding stuffed with stockings-full of festive yuletide cheer, holly, ivy, Perry Como, etc etc... you get the idea."

1986 had been a great year for this satirical puppet series which had peaked in both quality and popularity with an American adaptation for NBC and merchandise selling by the truckload including the No.1 Eurohit-spoof single "The Chicken Song", with lyrics from head writers Rob Grant and Doug Naylor, both of whom had since decided to leave the programme in order to work some sci-fi sitcom or other. For the remaining writing staff (headed by Ian Hislop and Nick Newman with future "Absolutely" men John – later Jack – Docherty and Moray Hunter) there was still much to be angry about in 1987; a magnificent Election special aired that June, immediately after the exit polls captured the hopelessness many felt at five more years of Thatcher.

This less topical but no more polite festive episode was the second one-off of the year and, if it doesn't quite scale the same heights, there are some great laughs nonetheless. Geoffrey Howe bores a filing cabinet at the Tory office party; a Fleet Street hack reworks the birth of Christ for the papers (*"Virgin In No Sex Baby Sensation! God Named In Baby Riddle Scandal"*); a desperate advert with a laugh in its voice nails the dire nature of Pantomimes (*"Cinderella, there'll be no more testicles for you!"*, *"Its 'balls', isn't it?"*, *"It certainly is!"*) and, to the delight of TV obsessives, there's a bit of cross-channel naughtiness with BBC One's fed up festive globe (*"When was the last time you saw snow on a Christmas pudding!?"*) The understandable lack of topical material due to the seasonal period meant lots more music, although sadly nothing as good as 1986's "Santa Claus is on the Dole", a minor hit as a follow up to "The Chicken Song". A spoof of Chas 'N' Dave's jaunty adverts for Courage Best Bitter becoming "Let's Go Drinking and Driving" (*"and put innocent lives at r-i-i-i-sk...."*) comes close though. Elsewhere, Perry Como is dreaming of a TV special just like the ones he used to get (*"When sleigh bells jingle / I release another single / for both of my fans who aren't dead yet"*) while Paul McCartney wishes he'd written "Imagine"[43] and Bruce Springsteen generally bums everyone out. There's also animation with the careless and disinterested "Temporary Postman Pratt" (*"and his student overdraft"*) and, in the episode's funniest moment, an unsurprisingly much shorter sequel to Raymond Briggs' classic with "The Snowman In The Kalahari". There are crap dated jokes about Michael Jackson dreaming of "a white Christmas" under the surgeon's knife and Rudolf's nose glowing due to being near the Sellafield nuclear site but they move along so fast it's hard to be bored.

Tuesday, 27th December, 1988

9.25am: T-Bag's Christmas Cracker (ITV)

"T-Bag hates Christmas and sets out to stop Santa Claus."

The first of four seasonal one-offs for Lee Pressman and Grant Cathro's naughty but fairly inept villain Tallulah Bag[44] and her press-ganged sidekick Thomas "T-" Shirt (played in every series by John Hasler). The characters normally appeared in a longer serialised format – all of which invariably including some torturous puns over tea or the letter T. "T-Bag's Christmas Cracker" finds the easily vexed witch attempting to stop Santa and swap his gifts for her own mind-controlling presents by travelling back in time to the home of an Edwardian family and pretending to be a nanny called...yes, "Merry Pippins". Ah, life really was so much simpler then, wasn't it...?

Wednesday, 27th December, 1989

---

43 I'd take "Wonderful Christmastime" any day over that dirge, Dinners!

44 Initially played by former Liver Bird and social worker Elizabeth Estensen (now a long-term resident of Emmerdale), she was replaced in 1990 by Georgina Hale as her sister Tabatha.

1.40am: Movie Premiere: Morons from Outer Space (ITV)

"When a section of their galactic holiday home is accidentally jettisoned into space, humanoid aliens from the planet Blob crash on to the M1 and are captured and fashioned into popstars..."

A peak time premiere! First released in cinemas in 1985 when Mel Smith and Griff Rhys Jones were one of the most popular acts in the country, "Morons" was critically planned and quickly forgotten, largely with good reason. Coming from the director of "Get Carter"[45] it has to be wondered where the fault although Jon Spira's terrific "Forgotten Film Club" book[46] interview with Griff suggests the script just wasn't up to scratch and Mel was rarely around to help rewrite it. The double act also don't actually meet until the final scene. It's a pity because there are both good laughs and fantastic ideas in there, spoofing the idea that aliens are always intelligent life forms in cinema, and with interesting points to make about the hollowness of celebrity. Mel Smith is genuinely brilliant in it and a natural performer who in another life would have been a great big-screen actor rather than director. The theme tune[47] is great too!

Friday, 27th December, 1991

---

45 Mike Hodges, who'd been working in the US but wanted to return home so agreed to direct on the condition his own "Mid Atlantic" was financed afterwards by Thorn EMI. Steven Paul Davies' Get Carter and Beyond: The Cinema of Mike Hodges (Batsford, 2002) has the quote: *"I found myself with a two-picture deal. It was too good to be true. And that's exactly what it was!"*

46 https://www.jonspira.co.uk/

47 Credited to The Morons but written by Mel with regular collaborator Peter Brewis. This got an official release on both 7" and 12" record via EMI but, like the parent movie, was not a hit.

9.50am Edd the Duck's Pantomime: Showbiz Edd and the Seven Dwarf Doods! (BBC One)

4.15pm: Jacks and the Beanstalk (BBC One)

"It's panto time with not one Jack but two!"

Two CBBC pantomimes for the price of NO. The first by Christina Mackay Robinson, a producer who usually had a hand in (or is that up?) the green haired puppet duck's appearances, is at least short and introduced by ship-jumping former CBBC presenter Andy Crane who for some reason is dressed as a goat. As for the rest its much as you'd expect with scenes such as Lesley Joseph asking *"who's the most showbiz of them all?"* into a mirror, which is answered by the Blue Peter presenters Yvette Fielding, Diane Louise-Jordan and John Leslie. Meanwhile Andi Peters plays a mobile-phone wielding dwarf called "Yuppie" who says *"ok yah"* a lot next to Nicholas Witchell's "Breakfast Newsie" ...I promise I'm not making this up!

"Jacks and the Beanstalk", screened later the same day, features some of the same names including Lesley Joseph on double duty as the Fairy Queen, yet more Andi Peters being incapable of speaking in a straight line, plus The Chuckle Brothers and Anne Charleston (as the "hilariously named" Madge the Neighbour). The script came from Jim Eldridge who seemed to write on everything when I was a kid including "BAD Boyes", "Spatz" and "Woof". Adults may know him from a million episodes of "King Street Junior" on Radio Four, a series I'm fairly sure nobody has ever listened to.

Monday, 27th December, 1993

7.00pm: At Home with Vic and Bob (BBC Two)

"Amid the detritus of wrapping paper, spent crackers and abandoned food, Reeves and Mortimer settle down to an evening of their favourite viewing in the living room of their elegant Victorian home."

Having made their name as a cult act on Channel 4, Vic and Bob had a lot to prove when moving to BBC Two. Your mileage may vary whether they were ever as good at the Beeb but, with many of their contemporaries long vanished from TV, it was a decision that undoubtedly cemented their thriving career as did one particular segment of this theme night featuring some of their favourite programmes from the archive including a newly made compilation of Eric Idle's terrific "Rutland Weekend Television", a rare 1972 Dad's Army sketch, the 1987 "Wildlife on One" documentary "Meerkats Utd" and, Mike Leigh's incredibly funny "Nuts in May", a "Play for Today" story from 1976 and one of the definitive looks at British holidays and manners. The evening also offered the chance for viewers new and old to encounter some characters devised for their just-screened series "The Smell Of Reeves and Mortimer" such as Pat Arrowsmith and Dave Wright who were two regular Northern fellers who just so happen to be wearing bras, plus appearances from troubled folk balladeers Mulligan and O'Hare and 1970s pop favourites Slade celebrating Christmas dinner in their family home with turkey flavoured Cup-A-Soups despite poncy, show-off cousin Simon Le Bon (Charlie Higson) and Ozzy Osbourne (Neil Morrissey) As well as these great new links and archive fun was a *"specially recorded quiz show"* starring Jonathan Ross, Wendy Richard and Martin Clunes taking on Danny Baker, Ulrika Jonsson and the real Noddy Holder. "Shooting Stars" seemed a bit knocked together but it was fun as a one off and, had BBC Two not needed a filler half hour to repeat in the following Spring, it would've stayed that way. When it got surprisingly decent ratings – much higher than any of the pair's sketch shows – BBC quickly commissioned eight episodes in 1995 with Ross replaced by troubled stand-up comedian Mark Lamarr. Totalling 72 episodes to date and two revivals, "Shooting Stars" may not be their greatest work but undoubtedly remains Vic and Bob's most enduring TV format.

Tuesday, 27th December, 1994

9.00pm: Fry and Laurie Host a Christmas Night with the Stars (BBC Two)

And Vic and Bob return to pester Sandie Shaw in this one-off attempted revival of the BBC's Christmas Day compendium of new sketches and scenes from the most popular series on both channels – originally broadcast between 1958 to 1972 – and most of which is now lost. Some of the surviving material was screened here, along with new sketches and stand-up from Two's current comedy line-up including the late, terrific Felix Dexter, characters from "The Fast Show", a chance to go Rambling with Alan Partridge, plus monologues from Alexei Sayle and Gregor Fisher as Rab C Nesbitt. Only the appearance of Ronnie Corbett nodded to the light entertainment of old which may explain the cool reception this one-off ultimately got, which vexed traditional audiences (in part due to Fry and Laurie's surprisingly smutty scripted links) or drew crowds of new comedy fans. BBC One made one more attempt at reviving the "Christmas Night with the Stars" format in 2003 but it was presented by Michael Parkinson so it doesn't count.

December 28th

"Jesus, are we still in that fecking Christmas?", you wail into the tinsel-bedecked hollow void you used to refer to as the living room. Christmas is over! A memory long forgotten of a person you used to be – happy, contented and covered in Quality Street wrappers – it's gotten so bad that next Christmas might as well be a year away!

At this point your brain is probably trying desperately to get you to actually do something, like sit up straight or move upright for over a minute. It's also good at reminding you of all the jobs you promised you'd get sorted after Christmas. But surely, it's still Christmas isn't it? There must be an answer in small print somewhere.

At least by now your relations should have hopefully buggered off to their own curled turkey sandwiches, meaning you can sit in the comfy chair Aunt Grandma stole the very first second you moved to go to the bathroom and hadn't moved from since. Not even to go to the toilet.

Oh. ...maybe you will just sit on the sofa instead.

And anyway, you can't do jobs as there's still new programmes and quality Shrek films on the television. Or at the very least a repeat of "Midsomer Hideous Death Crimes" or "Poirot In The Case Of The One That Was Much More Racist In The Original Book" that you haven't seen on ITV3. There! That's the spirit! Its December 28ʰ and, by golly, we're making the most of it. Pass the Dettol and a scrubbing brush...

Wednesday, 28th December, 1966

9.05pm: Alice in Wonderland (BBC One)

Whenever you hear about Jonathan Miller's adaptation of Lewis Carroll's classic story its invariably expressed in frothing 'its heavy, man!' psychedelic terms equating it to Pink Floyd, Aldous Huxley, "Performance" and Sgt Pepper's musical pals as part of some quiet revolution that the squares like totally didn't get. Less said is how fantastically well-made it is for someone who had never previously directed a film. Occasionally molasses-slow with manic flashes, Miller uses many of Carroll's original words to create a strange cloudy world between reality and fantasy, with a world of colour filmed entirely in black and white on gorgeous 35mm — a rarity for TV at the time which more commonly used 16mm film — and sound-tracked by the hypnotic sitar of Ravi Shankar. Some of your enjoyment may be tempered by the casting of newcomer Anne-Marie Mallik as the title character who plays the role as a constantly questioning regular awkward teenager who has seen it all and is impressed by nothing. She's aided by a cast full of brilliant names mixing darlings of the satire boom (John Bird and his former "Beyond the Fringe" colleagues Alan Bennett and Peter Cook playing Mouse and a brilliantly befuddled Mad Hatter respectively) and the old school (Wilfrid Brambell as the White Rabbit with John Gielgud, Michael Gough and Leo McKern.) Even Peter Sellers crops up for a small role as the put-upon King of Hearts.

Push the Disney 1951 version (and especially the rotten 2010 Tim Burton one) out of your mind and prepare yourself for a world that is tinged with fearful tones, preposterous characters and free thinking which builds to a wild and scary conclusion which seems much more in line with Carroll's original vision.

Monday, 28ᵗʰ December, 1970

4.10pm: Charlie Brown's Christmas (ITV)

"The wistful little comic-strip character with the spiral curl and the quizzical frown on a search for the real meaning of Yuletide."

That's "A Charlie Brown Christmas" to you mush, the still-joyful 1965 CBS TV special that brought to life the characters from Charles Shultz's Peanuts comic strip. What could be a schmaltzy mess is instead a funny, truthful take on how different people (or, in this case, surprisingly erudite eight-year-olds) feel about the holidays. Of course, there's some good old fashioned slices of American cheese in there – the kids all singing "Hark! The Herald Angels Sing!" around Charlie's awful Christmas tree for example – and even a bit of Jesus (courtesy of Linus quoting the Gospel of Luke) but it never feels preachy or forced. Best of all is the largely instrumental jazz soundtrack by the Vince Guaraldi Trio which remains one of those rare records that just radiates festive feeling in every note and gets around 5,000 plays every December in my house. It was even added to the US Library of Congress's National Recording Registry list of "culturally, historically or aesthetically important American sound recordings" in 2012. Good grief!

Wednesday, 28ᵗʰ December, 1977

3.30pm: Golden Great Hits of The Monkees (BBC One)

"When The Monkees split Micky Dolenz and Davy Jones teamed up with the songwriters behind many of their hits – Tommy Boyce and Bobby Hart – and here the four of them sing and talk"

Once considered throwaway and light, in recent years The Monkees' records have been re-evaluated as fantastic, playful and equal to many of their more fashionable contemporaries. They were completely out of step for this syndicated comedy and music special though which tried to recreate the magic of the original act with a new hybrid subtitled "The Guys Who Wrote 'Em and the Guys Who Sang 'Em". Despite a lengthy tour, lots of American TV appearances and an album full of original new songs, the public didn't take to the new act at all and they had quietly disbanded by the time this special aired.

9.00pm: Play of the Week – Our Day Out (BBC Two)

"One coach, 30 kids – and their teachers – set out from Liverpool to North Wales. Mirth and anarchy prevail while tempers flare."

This was the first airing of Willy Russell's comic play about a group of well-meaning but culturally trapped kids from Mrs Kay's Progress Class on a rare coach trip out. It was such a hit here BBC One quickly repeated it the following February as part of the prestigious "Play for Today" strand[48]. There was even a musical version which was first staged in 1983 - the same year that Russell's enduring classic "Blood Brothers" was also first performed. Comedy fans should note the actor playing the small role of zoo-keeper was Peter Tilbury who would go on to create the popular sitcoms "It Takes a Worried Man", "Shelley" and "Chef!"

---

48 On his website, Russell too looks back with great fondness claiming it took him less than five days to write basing much on his time teaching at Dingle Vale School in Liverpool: *"I still watch it today. The performances are exquisite. It just seemed to be one of those charmed ventures in which everything just fell into place."*

Friday, 28th December, 1979

5.15pm: The Solid Gold Top 20 (ITV)

"The best selling British records presented by pop's Jimmy Pursey."

POP'S JIMMY PURSEY?! A fine example to show The Kids who had been listening intently to the Truth from the middling 'punk' band he fronted – Sham 69 – whose original line-up had their fifth and final top twenty hit earlier in 1979 with "Hersham Boys" which, as we all know, went: *"Hersham boys / Hersham boys / Laced up boots and corduroys"*. Solid gold toss.

8.15pm: Kate (BBC Two)

"The most distinctive new sound of the 70s – that's Kate Bush"

Fasten your underpants dads as its time for 45 minutes by that lass in the leotard that nearly made you drop your crossword during "Top of the Pops"! With two albums already released, Kate Bush was a ridiculously young 21 when she recorded this strange but captivating special which gave the singer chance to experiment with the performance side of her already fairly theatrical act. Indeed, fans didn't know that in May 1979 she'd already performed her last full gig for 35 years. Bush previewed several new songs in this special despite her third LP 'Never for Ever" not being released until the following September, opening with "Violin" and also featuring "The Wedding List" and "Egypt". Its a well-chosen but mostly singles-free selection of songs from her back catalogue with only "The Man With The Child In His Eyes" cropping up near the end of the show. Sadly no "Hersham Boys" cover though...

Monday, 28th December, 1981

5.45pm: K9 and Company (BBC One)

"Christmas at Moreton Harwood. All is peaceful. Or is it?"

[Please note: The following capsule will be translated into "Serious Who fan" with subtitles on page 888.]

A daft but fun kid-centric spin-off from [SERIOUS DRAMA] *Doctor Who* that saw one of his most beloved companions Sarah Jane Smith, played by the terrific and much-missed Elizabeth Sladen, being gifted K-9 [ACTUALLY K-9 MARK III, NOT THE ORIGINAL MADE BY PROFESSOR MARIUS OR MARK II GIVEN TO ROMANA IN "WARRIOR'S GATE" ON 24/1/81] a special robot dog by Tom Baker's Doctor [PROBABLY BETWEEN SERIES 14 & 15, GIVING THE USUAL ALLOWANCES FOR UNIT DATING OF COURSE!!!] who arrives just in time to help solve a mystery involving kidnap and...ritual murder!??[!?!] With ratings better than its parent show [8.4 MILLION COMPARED TO 6.1 FOR THE FINAL TOM BAKER EPISODE OF "LOGOPOLIS"] it was expected by most to go to full series soon after, but this seems to have been knocked back due to a change of BBC One Controllers [ALAN HART, FORMER HEAD OF SPORT, REPLACED BY – SPIT – MICHAEL GRADE] and the new bod thinking it was a bit crap [WANTED TO DEVELOP NEW SHOWS.] Sarah Jane and K-9 would both return in the revived series of Who in 2006 – the popularity of which lead to an all-new and much more successful spin-off "The Sarah Jane Adventures". Sadly no space to discuss the theme by Fiachra Trench and superfan Ian Levine who is a bit of a knob [KNOB].

Tuesday, 28th December, 1982

8.45pm: Anyone for Denis? (ITV)

"While PM Maggie is away at a Euro-Conference, her husband Denis invites his drinking chums for a weekend of mischief at Chequers. But things go wrong when Maggie returns unexpectedly..."

One of many TV projects with a Private Eye connection, "Anyone for Denis?" was a stage farce by John Wells based on that magazine's incredibly successful series of spoof 'Dear Bill' letters – ostensibly written by Denis Thatcher to friend Bill Deedes, then the editor of The Daily Telegraph. The original stage production opened to huge acclaim at the Whitehall Theatre in 1981 minus the column's original co-writer Richard Ingrams who sniffily declined to take part fearing the worst. The Thatchers themselves had turned up to a charity performance of the show that July to try look half human, with Margaret telling a reporter through a plastered smile: *"We had a very enjoyable evening. It's a marvellous farce and I do think that the girl who played me, Angela Thorne, she's wonderful. She's obviously spent a tremendous time studying everything I do".* She was less sure of Wells' bumbling, boozy, slightly bigoted representation of 'im indoors, feeling it was *"not at all right".* The cast got chance to find out as they were invited to a function at Number 10 afterwards where Wells heard the Prime Minister's other half holding court about *'fuzzy wuzzies going on the rampage down in Brixton"* and suggesting *"the media are closet pinkoes".* Whether that included ITV who broadcast this play is anyone's guess but with the channel continuing through the eighties with the likes of "Spitting Image", "The New Statesman" and "Hot Metal", the public's desire to see politicians brought down a peg or two had never been more satisfied.

Wednesday, 28th December, 1983

5.15pm: Benji at Marineland (ITV)

"Benji is the first dog in the history of the world to attempt to scuba dive. Lana Afghana, Afghan newslady falls head-over-heels for him"

Also known as "Benji Takes a Dive at Marineland" this 1981 CBS TV special is a truly baffling mixture of disinterested real dogs, talking dog puppets, Calypso music and seemingly a lot of free advertising for a real Florida water park. Oh yeah and a NAZI DOG PUPPET watching from afar screaming he *"will never allow any Western Capitalist dog"* to become the first dog to *"scuba duba"* and plotting to take his place. Benji was everywhere in the 1970s and 80s including a flop Chevy Chase vehicle ("Oh! Heavenly Dog"), a Commodore 64 video game ("Benji: Space Rescue") and the dire fantasy drama series "Benji, Zax & the Alien Prince" which ITV seemed to show endlessly in my youth.

Saturday, 28th December, 1985

5.50pm: Watership Down (BBC One)

"When a young buck named Fiver has a frightening vision of their warren's destruction, a group of rabbits steal away to find a safer home."

And speaking of things that can piss off, here's the moment my childhood ended with the first showing on British TV of this well-made but horrific animated film, originally infecting cinemas in 1978. Myxomatosis couldn't come soon enough.

Sunday, 28th December, 1986

4.00pm: Aled Jones and Friends (BBC One)

"The 15-year-old Anglesey treble sings some of his favourite songs in a concert given to a packed St David's Hall in Cardiff."

Who knew that Aled Jones would turn out surprisingly normal and still be working for the BBC 30 years later? With Welsh as his first language, he didn't speak a word of English until he was six, but at 14 he had become pretty much instantly famous upon releasing his top five version of "Walking in the Air" from Channel 4's animated "The Snowman". I've always wondered how Peter Auty felt about Jones' fame considering its his (originally uncredited) voice in the cartoon and his version of the song flopped on initial release. And I'm not sure the entire BBC Welsh Chorus counts as "friends" Aled. And no, they definitely can't have a sleepover.

7.15pm: Penn and Teller Go Public (Channel 4)

"Penn and Teller, winners of this year's Golden Rose of Montreux will not only surprise your family and baffle your friends with their mind-boggling feats of legerdemain and prestidigitation, but they will also show how it's done. Or will they?"

If you only know Penn Jillette and Teller from their recent "Fool Us" series or the "Bullshit" documentaries, this 1985 show may surprise viewers with just how quickly it moves from the opening frame. Made for public TV (hence the title) station KCET in the US they make an instant impression as Penn reels off his complaints about the production team whilst rigging

Teller up in a strait-jacket and hanging him upside down, before insisting on reading the poem "Casey At The Bat" in front of him, still struggling to escape. It's exciting, different and a part of why they made such a mark when they appeared. Part of the early act was their reveal of how many tricks were done leading to outrage in the magic community. This only endeared them more to audiences who also enjoyed the more violent parts of their act which had sky rocketed in popularity between the taping and original airing of this special and even resulted in a 1989 film "Penn & Teller Get Killed". Channel 4 would later commission a six-part series entitled "The Unpleasant World of Penn & Teller", a fantastic and eye-opening programme that took the format of "Go Public" and ran even further into the macabre with it.

Wednesday, 28th December, 1988

9.00pm: French & Saunders Christmas Special (BBC Two)

"A Christmas special, very special, very Christmas, and you get ten minutes more for your money. Full of comedyness. gorgeousness and general all-round lovely snowy Christmasness."

I feel there are two types of people in this world – people who love French and Saunders and stupid wrong idiots.. This special was the first of seven festive shows they would make for the BBC and is full of great moments including the series' most controversial sketch to date with Jim and Jim – the comedians done up with fat suits to play dirty old men – paying "tribute" to the Queen. (*"Queen or no Queen – she's got wimmin's needs!"*) The piece led to complaints and the Tory MP Anthony-Beaumont-Dark demanded that an inquiry should be made. The most memorable segment however is the sublime spoof of Bananarama as Paula Yates attempts to interview pop sensations Lananeeneenoonoo, with Kathy Burke as third member Kim. The pastiches of the songs of the era produced by Simon Brint are note perfect and it's a testament to the popularity of the sketch, with both viewers and the band they were spoofing, that just two months later, all six would take part in 1989's Comic Relief single – a terrific rendition of The Beatles' "Help!" that manages to be funny and great pop music (The B-side "Love In The Factory" is very funny too.)

December 29th

When Roy Wood first press-ganged those poor schoolchildren into singing "I Wish It Could Be Christmas Everyday" it's a fair bet he wasn't thinking about December 29th - *"when you're still eating turkey / and there's frig all on the bo-o-o-o-x"*.

Reading back, I know I'm down on this post-Christmas Day period but that's mostly because, during this part of the year, my body almost always seems to take the opportunity to wave a white flag, declare itself on strike and fill me with flu, sickness and anything else that's going free. And as you'll learn from December 30th's entry that can put a real crimp in my plans because let's be honest — Christmas is about being social and the problem with being social is that it involves other people. And other people are filthy disease-ridden bastards, especially your family. Why was your nephew scratching so much at the dinner table? Did Uncle Jeff always have that cough? And what was that thing where the xenomorph burst out of your sister's chest and ran off down the road? She always has to show off.

So if you're still healthy and can feel both your legs, let the bells ring out for Easter. Or Summer. Or Shrek's bar mitzvah. Anything that isn't bloody bleedin' Christmas.

2.30pm: Out of School (ITV)

"A selection of schools programmes for teachers and others interested in education is being broadcast during the holiday."

Hey kids! You know all that school you're missing out on! Well have no fear because ITV are providing a special catch up service for all your "wishing you were dead" needs. One feature was Afternoon Edition in which kids around the country could phone in and speak to an expert like it was "Going Live!" but on sensible subjects you couldn't give a stuff about. The TV Times takes great pains to remind viewers that *"schools programmes are a highly specialised kind of television designed for a particular audience of a certain age range"* i.e. they're only fun if you're watching them instead of doing any actual work. Afterwards, as befitting the time exactly, television goes off air for an hour until "Crossroads" to think about what it has done.

7.30pm: The Best Of Hancock (BBC One)

"Hancock is upset by a steady stream of unpleasant letters."

"The Poison Pen Letters" was originally the final episode of Tony Hancock's sixth and last series under the title "Hancock's Half Hour" in 1960 which would return the following year five minutes shorter and shed of its regular support cast as simply "Hancock". Much is made of the ego clashes and seething jealousy with the other actors in the show in countless "sad 'Ancock" documentaries that have occurred since his demise by his own hand in 1968, but his partnership with Sid James in this episode really is a glorious thing to see and a template for all subsequent "social climbers dragged down by working class roots" sitcoms, including Galton and Simpson's own "Steptoe and Son" which followed once Hancock had buggered off to ITV without them. By the time of this best of run on BBC One, Hancock had already flopped with his next series. By the time of the following capsule in this book, he'd be dead.

Sunday, 29th December, 1968

6.30pm: Mother Teresa Has 5,000 Children (BBC One)

Does she? Must have been sore. This was a bonus pre-"Songs of Praise" Malcolm Muggeridge-produced religious special offering one of the first times many British viewers had learnt about Mother Teresa, something which seems ridiculous in the modern world where she is still the go-to comic reference for someone saintly. Muggeridge returned to this subject for a longer BBC Two documentary in 1969 where he claimed Teresa's "divine light" was visible on camera although most agree it was probably just some dodgy film stock.

Wednesday, 29th December, 1971

8.10pm: Man Alive (BBC Two)

"Zzonk! Eeeeefnu! Uurgh! Splat! - the world of Children's Comics"

If this programme was anything like some of the forums I've seen on the Internet in the past decade it will be mostly a 47-year-old man in his pants complaining *"comics should be exactly the same was they were when I was seven"* and, of course, *"It's PC gone mad! Dennis The Menace has even got a disabled in it now!"* In 1971, British comic sales were still big business. Not quite the numbers of the real boom in the fifties and sixties but with most titles easily reaching 300-400,000 sales per week with more for DC Thomson's flagship titles The Beano and The Dandy. The Radio Times capsule for this programme features quotes from everyone from Ringo Starr (*"I feel all the colleges were into the story sort of comic, and us plebs, we were all into the pictures"*) to George Melly (*"I think comics should be anarchic, should allow the child to feel it is in lovely secret revolt against its parents"*) The piece also featured the unnamed "Editor, Tammy" which referred to a then-new girls comic edited by 27-year old Gerry Finley-Day who would become synonymous later in the decade with his work on "2000AD" scripting many stories and co-creating the still-running "Rogue Trooper" series. Many of the sci-fi comic's staff had first worked on "Tammy" which the audience lapped up for a very respectable thirteen years until the comic came to a close in June 1984.

Friday, 29th December, 1978

4.15pm: Première for Elizabeth (ITV)

"The Royal Philharmonic Orchestra with the first public performance of 14-year-old Elizabeth Lane's Sinfonietta for Strings."

Another odd thing that you just couldn't imagine being broadcast now, Lane had appeared in a 1976 "Magpie" special called "And I Write Music" after winning the Dr Barnados / Nationwide "Champion Children" Competition. Now just Liz and a PHD, Lane continues to compose today.

3.30pm: Intergalactic Thanksgiving or Please Don't Eat the Planet (BBC One)

"A rock musical morality tale of space-age pioneer folk"

A surprisingly half-decent animated special about a family of humans who crash land on an alien planet with a hierarchy based on who is the funniest. The new visitors find that every ordinary thing they do is considered hilarious, and there's trouble in the air. This was Canadian company Nelvana's fourth special following 1977's "A Cosmic Christmas", "The Devil and Daniel Mouse" and the appallingly-titled "Romie-0 and Julie-8". Fans of all things bleeping and pointless will be delighted to know they worked on the animation for the infamous "Star Wars Holiday Special".

4.15pm: Watch It! (ITV)

"A new style for ITV children's programmes starts this week."

More kiddies fun with the first ever properly branded section for children on ITV which hoped to address the random scheduling of the various regions and provide more consistency. This first schedule featured the quirky cartoon series "Dr Snuggles"[49], the pilot for hobby based magazine show "FreeTime" with Mick Robertson and "The Book

---

49 "Dr Snuggles" featured several scripts by "Catweazle" and "Robin of Sherwood" creator Richard Carpenter plus two others co-written by "Hitchhiker's Guide" author Douglas Adams with his friend, the comedy production legend John Lloyd.

Tower" originally hosted by Tom Baker. The move proved to be popular but was still not fully available across the whole UK. The improved and fully linked Children's ITV launched on 3rd January 1983, two years ahead of the BBC's Broom Cupboard albeit with pre-recorded hosts.

7.40pm: Captain Beaky's World of Words and Music (BBC Two)

"A new television special based on the poems of Jeremy Lloyd."

An oddly scheduled family special depicting the adventures of "the bravest animals in the land" following a record, from which the title track, narrated by award winning Australian actor Keith Michell, became a top five novelty hit thanks to a glut of airplay by that wacky funster and Radio 1 presenter Noel Edmonds. Noel shows up here alongside Penelope Keith, Petula Clark, Peter Skellern and creator of the whole shebang Jeremy Lloyd, best known to modern audiences for co-creating "Are You Being Served?" and "Allo 'Allo!" As for Hissing Sid, rumours that he went into politics are as yet unconfirmed.

Tuesday, 29th December, 1981

9.00pm: The Three Sisters (ITV)

"The Royal Shakespeare Company's version of Chekov's classic about three tragic sisters living in a 19th century provincial town."

No, you aren't going dizzy from too much Captain Beaky. This was genuinely three-and-a-half hours of Chekov on prime-time ITV, directed by Trevor Nunn and featuring Suzanne Bertish, Roger Rees and Timothy Spall in the cast. Viewers hoping for a bit of light relief on the other side may have been horrified to discover that BBC One were showing Artemis '81, a visually interesting but utterly baffling three-hour science fiction play starring Hywel Bennett and Sting about the battle between good and evil for Mankind's future. Oh and its set on a ferry. Maybe an early night tonight then, eh?

Thursday, 29th December, 1983

4.45pm: The Sooty Story – The First Thirty Years (ITV)

"For the first time ever, Sooty has allowed the cameras behind the scenes to tell his story."

A celebration of Sooty, unveiled by impressionist Janet Brown – in character as Thatcher – who gives way to a series of vox pops between mildly confused real people (*"He played the piano...no, the xylophone!"*; *"I remember Ronnie Corbett was presenting it..."*) and celebrities...well, Bonnie Langford anyway. Despite these comic overtones, it's actually a fairly straight documentary featuring lots of lovely old clips from Harry Corbett's original BBC shows and later Thames programmes with son Matthew. Both are interviewed alongside behind-the-scenes footage and it serves to remind the viewer just how good they were with both puppetry and interaction with audiences. The most exciting part, however, shows Matthew composing on TWO KEYBOARDS AT THE SAME TIME! in his home recording studio which makes him look seriously bad-ass. Bye bye everybody, bye bye.

Saturday, 29th December, 1984

9.40pm: Come On Down! (BBC One)

"Barry Norman discovers American game shows – the liveliest, most outrageous programmes on TV. What makes a winner or a loser?"

From an era where clips of American television were incredibly exciting to see in the UK, those soft-focus over-lit gaudy visuals are everywhere in this tongue-in-cheek documentary about the great American game shows. Contestants and producers are interviewed and it goes behind the scenes of several series including "The Price is Right" which, earlier in 1984, had become a huge hit in Britain over on ITV.[50] Norman's appearance seems slightly perfunctory, presumably taking advantage of him being in the US for Film 84 duties and the tone of the show would probably benefit from a gentler touch but it's still a fascinating look at a slightly simpler world before coughing majors, Richard Osman's lol face and CJ from "Eggheads" allegedly murdering that man.

Friday, 29th December, 1989

2.00pm: The Little Match Girl (Channel 4)

Let's make one thing very clear from the outset – I despise Hans Christian Andersen's "The Little Match Girl" in which a happy ending is considered to be a child living in poverty freezing to death and being taken to Heaven. This 1987 NBC-produced TV movie eschews the whole dead child angle in

---

50 Viewers could actually watch the Christmas "The Price Is Right" with Leslie Crowther just before this documentary aired.

favour of casting Keshia Knight Pulliam (AKA Rudy Huxtable from "The [REDACTED] Show") as an angel who brings together warring 1920s socialites including William Daniels and Golden Girl Rue McClanahan. Another version of the story was made the same year in England by HTV featuring Twiggy and Roger Daltrey which gave the world the song "Mistletoe and Wine". Yeah, cheers for that "Hans".

Sunday, 29th December, 1991

7.15pm: Auntie's Bloomers (BBC One)

"Famous faces turning in performances they're unlikely to forget."

The first airing of Wogan's unmentionables as the BBC finally mounted a response to ITV's "It'll Be Alright on the Night". This cheery compilation of mistakes from "Auntie Beeb" shows quickly became a staple of the Christmas schedule, racking up over thirty editions until 2001 when it was replaced by "Outtake TV". Whilst much of the material was new to regular viewers for those working in television were familiar with clips due to private circulation of "Christmas tapes" - videos created by BBC staff for their end of year bashes — which combined bloopers with newly recorded sketches, songs and, worryingly, lots of nude tits. The talent soon got wise shouting *"Merry Christmas VT!"* every time something went wrong on set. Most of the original tapes on YouTube and worth a look although there's a strange eeriness to seeing context-free clips divorced of cosy presenters and without bleeps, not to mention the rather grubby nature of the material for the delectation of braying engineers plus baffling sketches and songs about "Pres Suite 2" and "VT Tea". What would Mrs Wogan say?!?

Tuesday 29th December, 1992

9.25pm: The Bogie Man (BBC Two)

"Francis is an escaped madman on the run who can hide behind multiple voices. Schwarzenegger, Connery or Humphrey Bogart."

A nice idea based on a small-press comic strip by Judge Dredd's creator John Wagner with Alan Grant and artist Robin Smith, Francis Forbes Clunie (Robbie Coltrane) is a Scottish mental patient who goes round solving mysteries that are invariably in his own head. Despite featuring Craig Ferguson and Midge Ure in the cast, The Bogie Man went no further on TV partly due to Coltrane not really nailing the madness of the character and partly because the creators had been kept out of the process of converting it to the small screen. This pretty much killed off Francis until 2005 when new story Return to Casablanca began in Judge Dredd Megazine.

Thursday, 29th December, 1994

9.50pm: Three Fights, Two Weddings and a Funeral – Pauline Calf's Wedding Video (BBC Two)

The second of two largely perfect and endlessly quotable video diary specials from Steve Coogan as violent student-hating pub philosopher Paul Calf and his fun-loving sister Pauline that should be in every self-respecting comedy fan's collection. Between the two specials, television had been introduced to the chat-astrophe that is Alan Partridge and fittingly, "Knowing Me Knowing Yule" also appeared on December 29th in almost the same time slot one year later.

December 30th

And lo it was after all that post-big day boredom that it was decided to send a child down to Earth whose birthday would be slightly rubbish falling between Christmas and New Year so nobody would want to come out to a party. And reader, that child was Shrek. I mean, me. Yes, not content with having a mother whose birthday is on Boxing Day, I have potentially the worst birth date in the world to boot as decades of "Oh can we just go out tomorrow instead?" have driven me to the brink of madness.

I entered this world officially at 12:12pm on Tuesday 30th December 1980 at a time where Saint Winifred's School Choir were number one and kids were flocking to see "Superman II", "Hawk the Slayer" and Nic Roeg's "Bad Timing" on the big screen. But what of the small rectangle? As I kicked and screamed my way into life BBC One were just finishing up a showing of Lassie tele-movie "The Miracle" before episode 71 ("Super Space Spies") of the confusingly re-edited Japanese adventure serial "Battle of the Planets". Meanwhile BBC Two were showing literally nothing because, other than the obligatory "Play School" at 11am, it could never much be arsed getting up before 4pm. Still that's better than Channel 4 which hadn't even had the good grace to be invented yet! Best of the bunch though were ITV who got ahead of the game with an episode of "Pipkins". And if my mother could have hurried up and birthed me 90 minutes earlier I could have arrived during a documentary on the same channel entitled "It's Hercules the Wrestling Bear"!

And if you're sat there thinking "Why should I care what was on when this git was plopped onto the miserable planet?" I agree but its December 30th! What the bloody hell else is there to talk about? A return to the Gold Standard? Watch yer telly and buy me a Twix already.

Tuesday, 30th December, 1969

10.30pm: Man Of The Decade (ITV)

"Which single personality has had the greatest effect on the Sixties? Could you name one man or woman who has had the strongest influence, for good or bad, over the whole world? Tonight three eminent people give their individual choice for the title and illustrate their nomination with film of the candidate in action."

A high minded popularity contest for the end of the year with broadcaster Alistair Cooke choosing John F Kennedy whilst at the other side of the spectrum Vietnamese revolutionary leader Ho Chi Minh was nominated by novelist Mary McCarthy. Most interesting however was Desmond Morris' choice of John Lennon who agreed to an accompanying interview near his Ascot home. Lennon made many interesting points about education and not fearing the possibility of peace, while clips were interspersed of The Beatles right through the sixties starting with their début from October 1962 for the Granada-only "People and Places" through to the bed in with Yoko who was also presented at the filming. It's strange to think that at this point Lennon knew The Beatles were officially done although it wouldn't become public knowledge until April the following year when McCartney officially announced he was leaving the group.

A Gallup poll of a thousand viewers were also asked to vote on their person of the decade with a list also featuring Sir Winston Churchill, pioneering heart surgeon Dr Christiaan Barnard, PM Harold Wilson and, because its only proper and British, Prince Charles, Prince Phillip and H.M The Queen. Personally, I think Rodney Bewes was robbed.

Tuesday, 30ᵗʰ December, 1980

4.45pm: Smith and Goody...On Ice! (ITV)

"Smith and Goody discover the wonderful world of presents, party games, pantomimes and nuts, which brings us back to Mel and Bob."

"Wotcha Bob!", "Wotcha Mel!" A leading contender for the show I haven't seen, but would most like to, was this children's literacy-based sketch show series. It paired Mel Smith with Bob Goody, both of whom had worked together in the late 1970s on various stage productions. The added joke in this final edition, a Christmas special, was that it really was partially recorded on ice, despite neither performer being able to actually skate. The double act stopped here, partially due to Goody's lack of interest in being a sketch comedy actor, but also because of the enormous success of "Not the Nine O'Clock News", from which a 45-minute compilation of the best bits from series three was shown the same day on BBC One. All of it went to show how magnificent a comic actor Mel Smith was and just why he'll be forever missed.

7.40pm: Showaddywaddyshow (BBC Two)

"One of Britain's outstanding rock 'n' roll groups. Nostalgia is their trademark and with they never seem to be out of the charts..."

...until about now. The 'waddywaddy had racked up fifteen top tens between 1974 and 1979 but their 1980 album "Bright Lights" had flopped hard, as would all of its singles. Luckily a great reception was guaranteed from the BBC Birmingham audience which was largely made up of members of the band's fan-club. Surprisingly, this was put out on DVD in 2009, minus special guest Kiki Dee, under the title "Greatest Hits – Live" and, as I type, a copy is presently yours on Amazon for just £329 (or pre-owned just £149.99). I think I speak for all of us when I say NO.

Wednesday, 30ᵗʰ December, 1981

1.30pm: I Really Want to Dance (ITV)

"When me Mam said ah'd got in ah wer all excited'... Philip Mosley, a 12-year-old from Barnsley. In this film combining documentary and ballet Philip describes the exhilarating but demanding process of learning to dance."

Whilst not a direct inspiration for "Billy Elliot", Mosley, who is still working in dance today and has long been associated with the Royal Opera House as a character artist, consulted with screen-writer Lee Hall for the 2000 smash movie about a lad who is secretly gannin oot dancin like wor puff bastaaad in 80s and not punchin a coppa in tha mush oor Biffa pie and a shite Jimmy Nail ah durnt want a medal for livin me life pet etc.

Friday, 30ᵗʰ December, 1983

3.50pm: Goodbye to The Good Old Days (BBC One)

"After 30 years of rollickingly rumbustious revelling risibility The Good Old Days roars to the end of its final run. We look behind the scenes at the world's longest running television variety show."

This recreation of Victorian music hall acts with modern day turns had been one of the BBC's staples since 1953. The announcement of its cancellation caused mild outrage at the time as this "Top of the Pops for people with ear trumpets" was still pulling big audiences, but it's easy in retrospect to see why it was a necessary move as the Beeb tried to drag itself into the eighties. This half hour, written and narrated by Barry Cryer, looked behind the scenes of the final show with contributions from Roy Hudd, Les Dawson and Larry Grayson. Repeats of "The Good Old Days" have resurfaced on BBC Four in recent years and Leeds City Varieties is a still very active and gorgeous venue, and I encourage every reader to visit at least once.

Saturday, 30th December, 1984

10.00pm: Weekend in Wallop (ITV)

"Nether Wallop has been missed by most of the great events of history. Henry V rode around it, Lady Godiva passed through it — dressed — but last September, everything changed, when the First Nether Wallop International Arts Festival was launched..."

Part-documentary, part-live show this is one of those wizard wheezes that could get funded once upon a time as a cast of thousands from the comedy, stage and music world descended upon a tiny Hampshire village for an all-new arts festival. High spots include Rik Mayall (who appeared both in character as Kevin Turvey, and also performing "Trouble", a favourite from the Comic Strip live shows, with the help of Jools Holland, Gilson Lavis and a shell-shocked Bill Wyman (sample lyric: "*I smoke marijuana and I don't go to lectures!*") Further music came via rock's two-hit wonder John Otway and his near-kamikaze take on "The Green Green Grass of Home". There's also a staggeringly pissed Peter Cook and Mel Smith as part of a *"tightly knit cabal of lesbians"* in a waterless synchronised swimming sequence, Fry and Laurie's Footlights-era sketch Shakespeare Masterclass and Rowan Atkinson as the frustrated Geordie coach of the Middle Wallop football team. The idea for the new festival originated with journalist Stephen Pile, who had rued in an article, the lack of anything historical ever happening to the tiny village. The manoeuvre seemed to work, and that same year Nether Wallop became the location of St Mary Mead in the new BBC adaptation of "Miss Marple".

Monday, 30ᵗʰ December, 1985

4.15pm: He-Man and She-Ra: A Christmas Special (ITV)

"He-Man and She-Ra and all their friends meet at the Royal Palace of King Randor & Queen Marlena for a gala Christmas party."

As an adult its easy to see just how unashamed 1980s cartoons were at being big toy adverts aimed at the under 10s. Better ask for all 372 characters and their variant models and big plastic box vaguely looking like a castle to shove them in or you may as well not turn up for school tomorrow, kids! A few of these shows suckered me as a kid but "He-Man and the Masters of the Universe" and the female targeted spin-off "She-Ra: Princess of Power" always left me cold thanks to bad animation, boring stories and really irritating characters. One such pain in the arse is Orko, a flying magic...thing, who is the catalyst for this story when a rocket sends him from usual setting Eternia to our very own Earth where he learns all about Christmas from some conveniently placed children. But not to worry – here's old painty can Skeletor to mess up He Man's plans and...wait, is he being licked by a robot puppy? He is. And he's...smiling!?! Goddamnit, you ruined Skeletor. And you don't even make a joke about him being made of bones! *"Blast it! I don't know what's coming over me... but whatever it is, I don't like it!"* You said it Skeletor mate.

Tuesday, 30th December, 1986

5.35pm: It's Not Just Zammo (BBC One)

Everyone remembers where they were when they saw Samuel 'Zammo' McGuire dead from drugs. Except they didn't... because he wasn't. Yes, his portly pal Roland did famously find his zonked out frame in the bogs of the arcade he worked at, but he was actually just passed out on account of being full of lovely drugs as opposed to doing a Danny Kendall. Eventually getting clean Zammo, played with great plausibility throughout the storyline by Lee MacDonald, manages to get his O-levels and even briefly engaged before leaving those famed school gates for "The Bill" and not much else afterwards. This "Newsround" special, presented by John Craven with Nick Ross, had originally been shown in April 1986 as part of the BBC's "Drugwatch" campaign and continued to open eyes for the nation's 9-year olds who never even knew what drugs were. After that came "Just Say No", a finger-wagging pop morality groove sung by members of the cast which made it to No.5 in the UK charts and famously led to a visit to the White House in Washington DC for a very well-publicised meeting with the similarly moralising First Lady Nancy Reagan who was spearheading the hugely successful War on Drugs which stopped all drugs for the rest of history. *"I gave her a copy of the record, which she swiftly threw underneath her chair"*, MacDonald told the *Radio Times* in 2015. History does sadly not recall her reaction to the follow-up single "You Know the Teacher (Smash Head)". Pass the tinfoil...

Sunday, December 30th, 1990

5.50pm: Living with Dinosaurs (Channel 4)

"Dom is the 10-year-old son of a sculptor father and a hardworking, heavily pregnant doctor mother. Relationships are strained and Dom's toy dinosaur is the only one he can trust."

For a programme worked on by the Jim Henson Organization, written by future Oscar winner Anthony Minghella, directed by Paul Weiland, produced by Duncan Kenworthy and starring Juliet Stevenson you'd think more people would have heard of this sentimental one-off story. This might be in part to it being co-produced by TVS Films – a branch of the ITV region Television South who had previously had a hand in bringing *Fraggle Rock* to the screen. After TVS lost their licence in 1992, their output came to be owned, via a complicated series of mergers and buyouts, by Disney (who amazingly have better things to do than sift through their vast archives for *All Clued Up* repeats). *Living with Dinosaurs* is a well-written if slightly downbeat show but very representative of the boundaries Jim Henson was trying to push, right up until his tragically early death in May 1990.

December 31st

Last New Year, just as the Eve had safely stumbled into New Year's Day, I was getting a taxi home having played music at people in my town's only alternative music venue, which meant being out and awake until 5am. As I made my way home, I could see the full aftermath of my small town's explosion of forced celebration, abandoned takeaway food and regurgitated neon drinks. When did it all get so bleak?

Looking back over all these old TV listings has made me nostalgic for a time that I don't really remember and probably never actually existed, where people would have family get-togethers, eat haslet sandwiches, and play the modern tunes of the day on piano such as "Don't Put Your Daughter in a Lead-Lined Container Full of Barium, Mrs Worthington", "The Harold Wilson Rag" and "All Star (Love Theme From Shrek)" by Smash Mouth. I've always been quite envious of Hogmanay where friends and strangers unite to toast the New Year with tradition and love and occasionally setting fire to things. It's not just about which pub is allowed to stay open the longest and what takeaway will keep its windows intact until January 2nd.

To properly look at the occasion of New Year via the eyes of TV I've separated this into two sections. The first section looks at some of the general programmes that were on during 31st December. It's followed by an essay on the shows that were actually scheduled to see in the coming year from the fifties to the nineties. What years did Kenny Everett get full control of the Thames celebrations? Did BBC One really show a new "EastEnders" at 11:30pm? Which listed guests failed to appear on "Come Dancing with Jools Holland"? All the answers and much more can be found as the clock strikes 12...

Saturday, 31st December, 1966

6.15pm: The Monkees (BBC One)

"A new film series starring Davy Jones, Peter Tork, Micky Dolenz and Mike Nesmith who find the deck stacked against them..."

With two number one hits in America and an equally successful first album, the UK finally got chance to see what all the fuss was about with the first episode of the prefab four's sitcom airing just five months after its US début and featuring a typically daft high concept plot (*"The Monkees rescue Princess Bettina, Duchess of Harmonica from her evil uncle Archduke Otto"*) alongside some of the best pop music of the whole sixties, with "Take a Giant Step" the highlight of this first episode. An accompanying article in the Radio Times asked, "What do the Monkees want?" to which the reply was, *"To be free... to make every day Saturday night, to climb impossible mountains, to take a trolley car to the moon, to deflate stuffed shirts."*[51] It clearly had an effect on its target audience; within three weeks "I'm a Believer" would reach No. 1 staying there for four weeks, during which time follow-up single "Last Train to Clarksville" entered the chart. Four more big hits would follow in 1967 and the TV show remained part of BBC One's Saturday night line-up for most of the year. The Monkees were smart, knowing and funnier than critics tend to give them credit for, so you'd better get ready because they may be comin' to your town...

#Here they come / walking down the street / after Doctor Who's 'The Highlanders' / which is at Part Threeeeeeeee....

---

51 Presumably *"to be repeated endlessly on increasingly terrible quality film prints right into the 2000s"* was next on the list.

Sunday, 31ˢᵗ December, 1972

10.35pm: Up the Channel (BBC Two)

"A last half-hearted stand before entry."

A special episode of the late night arts 'n' satires show "Up Sunday" as Kenny Everett, William Rushton and John Wells look at Britain's imminent joining of the European Economic Community the following day – another thing that probably seemed much funnier before we buggered that all up. The move into Europe was controversial but was greeted by many with warmth and excitement at becoming part of something bigger, and nowhere more so than at BBC Radio who the following day went Euro-potty with debates, concerts and musical guests from across the water. Radio 1 even sent out its entire daytime line-up: Tony Blackburn presented his breakfast show from Luxembourg, followed by Jimmy Young live in Brussels, Dave Lee Travis in Cologne and Alan Freeman in Rome! Shame they all came back really...

Monday, 31ˢᵗ December, 1973

8.00pm: Love Thy Neighbour (ITV)

"No traditional New Year's Eve for Eddie and Bill - they are forced to work, leaving Joan and Barbie at home alone."

A sitcom of indescribably bad taste, yet with huge ratings, that hid behind the lame fact that the weekly half hour of racist taunts the white character Eddie Booth casts towards his black neighbour Bill were okay because nobody took him seriously. I did try watching this whole episode of Vince Powell and

Harry Driver's sitcom but despite a genuinely great cast and despite relatively little racially insensitive material on display (although Eddie buys Bill *"a bottle of hair straightener"* for Christmas to insane audience laughter) it remains an utter slog. This is because, even with Bill (Rudolph Walker) being equally argumentative back, Jack Smethurst's bigoted lazy motor-mouth union leader Eddie is just too unpleasant to spend time with. This element of the show would later affect the fortunes of Smethurst, who unfortunately struggled to get further acting work after the series ended in 1976.

Wednesday, 31ˢᵗ December, 1975

7.50pm: Three Men in a Boat (BBC Two)

"The three men, not forgetting the dog, set out on their epic voyage of mishap up the Thames."

An all-star adaptation of Jerome K Jerome's timeless tale with a script adapted by Tom Stoppard, direction from Stephen Frears and the titular three men played by Tim Curry, Stephen Moore and Michael Palin wrote about the experience fondly in his essential collection of diaries "The Python Years" which also contains his attempt to watch it go out live with a house full of New Year guests including children *"a long way from the sitting still and shutting up age"* making it difficult to hear as *"Stephen has opted for a very gently paced, softly played treatment which seems to be at least ten decibels quieter than any other TV shows."* The following week BBC Two would broadcast Palin and Terry Jones's savage take-off of old-fashioned literary "boys school" adventures "Tomkinson's Schooldays" which would become the first episode of the terrific "Ripping Yarns".

Friday, 31ˢᵗ December, 1976

7.00pm: Bruce's Choice (BBC One)

"Bruce Forsyth invites you to join him as he watches one of his favourite editions of The Generation Game with Anthea Redfern"

This is included here just to evoke the delightful mental image of Brucie sat in his nicely appointed living room, gently beckoning you to join him on the settee with a box of Quality Street on the go whilst Anthea makes a brew. Then he goes and talks over the top of it, telling you the best bits and when the old woman was going to fall over. Still it's better than when he insisted on watching "Takeover Bid". The theme song doesn't even make sense, Bruce! *"I'm gonna be the first on the grid to take over you"*? You're mixing your metaphors!

Sunday, 31ˢᵗ December, 1978

6.00pm: Matt the Goose-boy (BBC Two)

"Matt is a boy who finds himself pitted against the village landlord, Lord Blackheart; and all because one day Blackheart tries to deprive Matt of his best friend and constant companion... a goose."

Wait, is this a real thing or did I make it up? It's an animated film based on an epic narrative poem called "Mattie the Gooseboy" (or Lúdas Matyi in the native language) by Mihály Fazekas, you say? With music by Franz Liszt? And was a 'HUNGAROFILM' production?! Of course, that explains it. In other news, I would like to go home now.

Friday, 31st December, 1982

7.40pm: The Keith Harris Show (BBC One)

"Start your New Year with a bang as Keith Harris brings you comedy, music and dance with special guests Bucks Fizz."

See, it was always Keith's show, never yours, you little green bugger. After appearing on every variety series going for the best part of a decade, Harris was finally awarded his very own programme just as his dire saccharine ballad with the bird, "Orville's Song", was going up the charts[52]. Sadly that record seems to have been the noose around the genuinely talented Harris's neck as his act slipped more into kiddy fare, with the popular Orville taking over much of the material from the much funnier and naughtier Cuddles the Monkey. Indeed, Cuddles shared many of our sentiments when he frequently described his displeasure for the duck. It's a pity as Keith was a genuine talent and whilst a bit cheesy and trad by modern standards, this special's opening song and dance version of "Can You Feel It?" at least showcases his enthusiasm to entertain, and doesn't utilise either puppet until the very end when they appear, hands free, to heckle him.

8.00pm: Russ Abbot's Hogmanay Madhouse (ITV)

"Live from Invercockaleekie Castle in Bonnie Scotland, 'Jimmy' and his family open the doors of their ancestral home. So hang on to your haggis, slacken your sporrans and keep a firm grip on your caber."

---

52 At the time this episode went out the song was at No.33 in the charts, eventually climbing up to No.4 in January.

Recently I had the "privilege" to see an episode of "Freddie Starr's Variety Madhouse" from December 1979 in which Russ Abbot played second banana to the once-anarchic but awkward title star and is as you'd expect diabolical with Starr doing his usual mix of pretending to be Hitler and shouting but Abbot clearly the real star from the get go with a naturally comic personality and the ability to make the lame scripts at least seem slightly alive. It's no surprise then that when Starr buggered off Russ was bumped up to the title role for eventually six series and a bunch of specials including this episode based around his most popular character – the over the top and near incomprehensible Scotsman C U Jimmy – usually found as host of the now somewhat verboten "Jim'll Jinx It" slot. And, yes, ginger wigs and kilts unsurprisingly abounded throughout.

Speaking of incomprehensible Scotsmen…

Sunday, 31ˢᵗ December, 1989

9.30pm: Rab C. Nesbitt's Seasonal Greet (BBC Two)

"'See me, see you, see Christmas?' Naked Video's bandaged philosopher explains why the festive season makes him no-well."

This was the first chance viewers outside Scotland got to see the extended world of Govan's *"original unemployed person"*. This Greet had been held back a year since its original BBC Scotland showing on 21ˢᵗ December 1988. The alcoholic, highly-opinionated and strangely lovable Nesbitt had quickly become one of the breakout characters of BBC Two's sketch series "Naked Video", with his fiery first person monologues played perfectly with a mixture of righteousness and self-defeat by

Gregor Fisher. The straight-to-camera style of his early appearances is combined with more traditional sitcom scenes; Rab wanders the high street railing at the modern Christmas and trying to convert a Salvation Army collector into giving it all up and letting doubt into her life (*"Be a Devil, give atheism a try!"*) before heading home to his pregnant wife Mary and continuously scrapping sons Gash and Burney, who are still fairly rough sketches of the richly drawn, fragile and identifiable characters they would come to be. Ian Pattison's terrific scripts deserve to be rated on a par with contemporaries John Sullivan or Simon Nye. The first full run of "Rab C Nesbitt" began in September 1990 and continued right through the decade until 1999 before returning for two very welcome further series in 2010 and 2011. BEAT IT!

Monday, 31st December, 1990

10.20am: Paddles Up (BBC One)

"Television's international canoeing competition, for the Norwich Union Trophy on the River Tryweryn at Bala, Wales. Great Britain take on paddlers from Sweden, the Netherlands, Belgium and Italy."

Paddles up what? The BBC were a big fan of their sporting trial shows with the likes of "Kick Start", "Britain's Strongest Man" and for people who like doing shit in canoes "Paddles Up" which had an impressive run between 1983 and 1993. This series saw the British contingent walloped by the 23 year old Dutchman Michael Reys who would go on to compete for his country in canoe slalom in 1992 and in 1996 where he came eleventh both times. See, you can't say you don't learn owt from this book.

Thursday, 31st December, 1992

6.30pm: That's Showbusiness New Year's Eve Show 1992 (BBC One)

"Two teams of celebrities take a wry look at the last 12 months of show-business including Madonna's book, Michael Jackson's nose and Michael Douglas's extremely basic instincts."

What a wonderfully no messing about title for this 1992 special which presumably was mostly about Carter USM's "1992 The Love Album". With special guests Lesley Joseph and Keith Barron both saying it's a bit bobbins and not a patch on "101 Damnations" (although "Do Re Me" was a good single.)

9.25pm: The Doug Anthony All-Stars (BBC Two)

"Music and comedy from Australia's most irreverent trio."

Some acts arrive on the scene with a flourish, some with a bang. The Doug Anthony All-Stars arrived with three pounds of gelignite and a photograph of your sister in the bath. Trading a fine line in all-purpose offensiveness – frequently in extremely catchy musical form – the Australian three piece had been a huge hit at the Edinburgh Fringe and turned up regularly on UK shows. But whilst their homeland had offered them a series[53] this special was the only show they got to headline in the UK. Regardless, the trio packed the half-hour tight like a condensed

---

53 The fun if uneven sketch / sitcom hybrid "D.A.A.S. Kapital" (two series, ABC, 1991-92)

cluster-bomb which, even toned down a little, still feels fearless with the censor-baiting "Funk You" at the top of the show setting out the stall for viewers new and old. (*"Funk you/ Funk quantum physics / When you've proved their theories wrong / You can go and funk the cynics / Take a proton pill as you butt funk their gimmicks..."*) Watching today some of the jokes and dives for the shock button can seem a little forced but the interplay between the three performers pushes beyond that. Paul McDermott plays the angry, impotent front-man, Tim Ferguson the cute but easily led sidekick and Richard Fidler on guitar as the put upon, naive one. There's also room for bald yet kiss-curled support act Flacco whose strange, cerebral act mixed with an accent-from-somewhere-vaguely-European clashed enjoyably with the deliberately styled coolness of the headline act. And DAAS were genuinely bona-fide, pin-up poster cool, more like a rock act than a comedy troupe which lead to leagues of young screaming fans similar to our own contemporary acts Newman and Baddiel or the late Sean Hughes which led to many tears when the Dougs called it a day in 1994. The reason they gave was that the act had simply come to an end and all three wanted to live in different places due to their success both in England and Australia. Later, Ferguson would reveal the split was in large part due to his worsening health issues, which would develop into multiple sclerosis, consequently affecting the trio's incredibly physical live act. So it was a surprise when Paul and Tim announced an official return in 2013, with Fidler replaced on guitar by the man behind Flacco's curl, Paul Livingston, for a new show based around the fact they're no longer young or sexy and Paul is the miserable caretaker of Ferguson whom he assumed would be long dead but instead permanently in a wheelchair. Selling out at the Edinburgh Fringe in 2017 it feels like things have come full circle for the Doug Anthony All-Stars. Long may they continue to funk.

And so we move on to the evening which before catch-up and video recorders was a strange hinterland for schedulers. People staying in want to be entertained but most people are going out so don't want to miss anything good. Here's my condensed look at how telly covered the Buckfast and tear-stained New Years, from the fifties through to the nineties...

The Days Of Black And White

Ever since 'Itler and his fascist hordes were sent packing, the BBC were ready to party... in respectable clothing and headwear of course. Having resumed TV broadcasts in June of **1946**, that December 31ˢᵗ became one of the first times television had comfortably gone past the witching hour as *"Viewers in their homes are invited to take part in the festivities in the Ballroom at Grosvenor House with Charles Adey and Dawn Leslie Strange and Sidney Lipton and his Orchestra"*. So, drop a tab of rationed Oxo and let's go shag some airmen! Later years would offer a link up to St. Thomas's Hospital in London and, as soon would become tradition, Glasgow for the Hogmanay celebrations.

1956 was the first year to get a little more adventurous as *Where's There's Life...* found Raymond Baxter stick his beak into celebrations everywhere, with piping in Scotland, working men in The Midlands, pilots in Wales, band-leader Ted Heath at the Chelsea Arts Ball, "the Continent" where *"midnight strikes one hour ahead of us in time"* at sea, and most excitingly "A West Indian Party" where newly arrived families *"get together in London for a rhythmic New Year's Eve to the beat of the Trinidad All-Stars Steel Band, the Calypso chants, and the Caribbean Music of Hugh Scotland."* Our next big moment sees us take to the early minutes of **1959** with the first New Year's edition of the traditional Scottish variety series *The White Heather Club* from the BBC's television studios in Scotland, although tartan purists may be alarmed to note that regular host Andy Stewart was not yet a feature of the programme. All the same there's plenty much time for The Joe Gordon Folk Four, The Andrew Macpherson Singers and The Gie Gordons. And viewers may wish to know that Robert Wilson is appearing at the Tivoli, Aberdeen; Jimmy Logan is in "Sinbad the Sailor" at the Alexandra Theatre, Glasgow, and Alistair McHarg is in "Mother Goose" at the King's Theatre, Edinburgh.

The newfangled BBC Two saw in its first new year (**1964**) with the grooviest party in town as its regular *The Beat Room* series ran the special *Beat In The New!* with Billy J Kramer and The Dakotas, The Merseybeats and PJ Proby just a few of the names who helped the youngsters of the day rock and roll around their 12" black and white Pye television sets. Clearly this was seen as a challenge over on ITV, and on the last day of **1965**, at the exact time of 10.52pm, pop suddenly happens with *The New Year Starts Here* which makes the competition's continuing mix of Hogmanay honking pipes and homosexual Gordons suddenly seem awfully naff next to a line-up of The Animals, Tom Jones, The Kinks, Dave Clark Five, Lulu, The Rolling Stones, The Who and more, as *"the most exciting New Year's Eve Party in Britain is at Television House. London, where the stars go to dance to the music of the top popsters."* Hosted by Keith Fordyce and Cathy McGowan of Rediffusion-era ITV's pop show *Ready Steady Go!*, this was a spin-off in all but name.

BBC One's new year party stayed in Scotland for the next few years but they did manage to sneak in a pre-midnight treat for the young types with **1967**'s confusingly titled *Suddenly It's 1968* hosted by the man of the moment Simon Dee whose twice-weekly *Dee Time* chat show (or *"early evening scene"*) was the hippest programme in town. Here he was the face of a New Year's Eve Party from The Talk of the Town in London including Julie Felix, The Alan Price Set and erm... Roy Hudd, who to be fair was still only 75 back then. By the end of **1968** however Dee was down to one show a week and would soon leave the Beeb over money, and so *Cilla* was in although the guests were equally unusual, with Matt Monro and Billy Cotton, plus The Irving Davies Dancers as standard. Frankie Howerd was on hand, though, to offer a bit of tittering into next year with a script courtesy of Ray Galton and Alan Simpson who pretty much owned comedy in the 1960s.

Lulu's back again in **1969** but over on ITV who have got in on the National Scottery with a *Hogmanay Party* and shock waves as Andy Stewart has also switched channels after the demise of *The White Heather Club* to celebrate the opening of The Gateway – Scotland's first ever colour television studio. Scotland's first ever colour television set is expected to be sold in 2024. Baboom tscch. Meanwhile on BBC One there's more Jesus and Scottishery after midnight (*"starring Moira Anderson"*) but it's preceded by **Pop Go the 60s!** a co-production between the BBC and ZDF in West Germany featuring performances from many of the same acts from ITV's earlier 1965 chart-bound shindig. Here, though, there's added Beatles appearing alongside the unusual musical bedfellows, with support from The Bachelors, Cliff Richard, Marmalade, Horst Jankowski, Kenny Ball and his Jazzmen, Sandie Shaw and bloody Lulu again. Filmed at BBC Television Centre, the introductions were done for both countries with Elfi Von Kalckreuth speaking only in German, whilst the English links came via a scrawny old sex offender whose name I won't trouble you with but should definitely have fallen into a large, deep well more.

Swing Into the Seventies

The beat went on in **1970** with Elton John, Traffic, Labi Siffre, Livingston Taylor, CCS and Bloody Lulu going *Into 71* but for the actual midnight hour the Beeb decided it was high old time that we return to *The Good Old Days* which excitingly is a live edition from Leeds, although less excitingly it features Norman Wisdom. ITV continues with Andy Stewart in *The Hogmanay Show* as he's joined by Dana and the much loved yet baffling South outside Scotland duo Francie and Josie played by Jack Milroy and Rikki Fulton, the latter of which would soon become a huge part of the Scottish New Year's celebrations.

Before the BAFTAs got ideas above their station one of the top award ceremonies on TV was The Variety Club Awards at which the children's charity honoured British entertainers and between **1971** and 1974 this was incorporated into BBC One's *Top Of The Year* hosted by Michael Aspel. Over on the commercial channel, they were largely sticking with the tartan-taste of the first-footing variety but did up the show-biz factor with **1972**'s cheekily titled *At Last The 1973 Show* hosted by David Frost and featuring a lot of "we can sell this to America" names like Stubby Kaye, Eartha Kitt and Ethel Merman alongside our own Jimmy Edwards, Stanley Baxter, Peter Cook and Dudley Moore. **1973's** special replaced David Frost and London for *New Year's Eve at the Golden Garter* and Manchester presented by the just as Frost-like Bernard Manning. Already well known for his appearances on moribund stand-up vehicle "The Comedians" and soon to star as compère of the fictional *The Wheeltappers and Shunters Social Club* which would launch the following year and, despite its rather tacky nature, would quickly get its own New Year's Eve specials in **1974** and **1975** due to its huge popularity at the time.

After a few years of just settling back and showing a film BBC Two returned to the post-Big Ben bongs beat in the opening minutes of **1974** with the first New Year compilation of the serious music for serious people programme ***The Old Grey Whistle Test*** which would become a regular fixture until the late 80s and much appreciated by younger viewers who would otherwise be stuck with the likes of **1975**'s ***For Auld Lang Syne*** on BBC One where the highlights seem to be *"Max Boyce joins the crew of the Mumbles Lifeboat for an informal get-together at The Pier Hotel"* and that still-disgraced paedophile bothering people at Stoke Mandeville like bloody usual. He's back in the following year's ***Welcome 1977*** too alongside *"New Year's greetings from BBC stars Kojak, Starsky and Hutch, Petula Clark and from the Armed Services worldwide"* which is probably why they brought back ***The Good Old Days*** for **1977** and **1978**.

The move away from pop to light entertainment continued as the final hours of **1979** were, like 1969, given to a retrospective, but this time it celebrated the great television of the decade as Penelope Keith introduced ***The 70s Stop Here!*** with highlights of *"some of the BBC programmes which achieved popularity, esteem or even notoriety during the decade."* Amongst the many names featured in clips were John Hurt, the cast of "Dad's Army", Derek Jacobi, "The Goodies", Michael Parkinson with his pals Rod Hull and Emu, Dr Jacob Bronowski, Larry Grayson, Morecambe and Wise and the Wilkins Family of Reading who'd been part of one of the first fly-on-the-wall documentaries The Family in 1974 – a series that had been cruelly lampooned in the "Most Awful Family In Britain Contest" sketch by the Monty Python cast. The Pythons, who also featured in this show, had experienced a fascinating 1970s, graduating from post-11pm obscurity to household names and were just at his point entering into "Life of Brian" infamy.

For those who preferred their Auld Lang Syne with a bit less of the auld, ITV provided *The 'Will Kenny Everett Make It To 1980?' Show* with guests The Boomtown Rats, Cliff Richard, Roxy Music, and David Bowie – who performed a stripped down semi-acoustic version of "Space Oddity" which would be used as the basis for his video to 1980 No. 1 "Ashes to Ashes". One of Kenny's best ever shows, this full hour has guests on great self-effacing form and a genuine sense of a great party viewers were invited to, topped off by a well refreshed super-group of Thin Lizzy and Sex Pistols singing various Christmas tunes. Ken was invited back the following year for *The Kenny Everett New Year's Daze Show* before scheduling disputes saw him move to the BBC just in time for Christmas 1981.

Eighties, Push, Push, Struggle

The TV retrospective theme established in 1979 was continued with *Pick of 80* and *Pick of 81* hosted by Barry Took that showed clips from... well, you can probably guess that. *The Good Old Days* was once again given the 11pm slot in **1980**... except for viewers in Scotland who, rather than the usual Paul Coia quiz show about hills or a six-part cartoon series about Gaelic accidents, got the first *Scotch and Wry* special, a sketch show vehicle for Rikki Fulton that would become a permanent fixture in the pre-midnight slot in Scotland very year until 1992. Only one year was skipped – the very next one, **1981** – which went with another BBC Scotland production *81 Take 2* although this was shown across the full UK. It featured many of the cast of BBC Two's new sketch show "A Kick Up the Eighties" including Rik Mayall, Robbie Coltrane and Celia Imrie with guest performers including Chic Murray and The Hee Bee Gee Bees which, as it sounds, was indeed a spoof of the Bee

Gees courtesy of Angus Deayton, Michael Fenton-Stevens and Phil Pope. The trio had been part of the Oxford Revue team, and their spoof of commercial radio had led from a live show at the Edinburgh Fringe to the long-running Radio 4 series "Radio Active" which had finished its first series.[54] Still in 1981, after Big Ben's chimes we DON'T return to Scotland for the first time in years. Instead we head for Pebble Mill in Birmingham for *Hi There 82!* which undid any cool from the previous programme by scheduling Danny La Rue, Andy Williams, Norman Collier and Wall Street Crash, *"with a little help from the Hi-De-Hi! team."* I hope it's help into a big burning bin.

1982's New Year offerings were so dull as to be almost unmentionable. BBC One ran yet more bloody *The Good Old Days* followed by *Across The Years* hosted by John Craven and *"organised by the English Tourist Board"* before the equally exciting *The Big Ben Band Show* from Birmingham as Syd Lawrence and his Orchestra were joined by Tina Cross and Shakatak for *"an informal but exciting mixture of music, comedy and nostalgia"*. ITV continued with *The Hogmanay Show* but there was however a new kid on the block, as the all new Channel 4 had just been launched and was full of exciting new presenters, interesting programming and a different way of thinking. So quite how that led to *David Frost's End of the Year Show* with guests like Jonathan Dimbleby, Esther Rantzen and Nigel Dempster is a baffling mystery. Frosty was back on C4 in **1983** too, opposite Keith Chegwin on BBC One, creaky horror flick *Theatre of Blood* on BBC Two and Kenneth McKellar with the Scottish Fiddle Orchestra on ITV, but by **1984** he had been replaced by Julia Migenes-Johnson

---

54 A special entitled *The Hee Bee Gee Bees Story* had also been broadcast by Radio 2 on December 19th 1981.

with *"a selection of songs from operetta, classical and music show favourites"*.

Whistle And I'll Come At You

Having gone through a slightly awkward transitional period, where it lost original host Bob Harris and *The Old Grey* bit of its original title, *Whistle Test* was back back BACK for New Years Eve **1984** with *84 Whistle Test 85*, a whole evening of live music including Nik Kershaw at the Hammersmith Odeon and Big Country keeping up the mandatory Scots content live from Edinburgh. The evening expanded to five and a half hours in 1985 for the imaginatively titled *85 Whistle Test 86* which reflected the team's big achievement that summer in *The Band Aid Story* and clips from Live Aid. More live music came from Madness in London and King in Glasgow. And in a blaze of technological achievement viewers could tune into Radio 1 simultaneously and create a stereo broadcast. On to *86 Whistle Test 87* and BBC Two was now clearly the place to be for the discerning rock fan, with concert footage from the eclectic line up of The Police, Jean-Michel Jarre, Kim Wilde, Suzanne Vega and Level 42, plus more Live Aid in the documentary *Africa Tomorrow*. The evening ended at half twelve with the first showing of D. A. Pennebaker's 1973 film of *Ziggy Stardust and The Spiders from Mars*, documenting the farewell performance of Bowie as Ziggy. Sadly **1987** was to be the final year the whistle blew as the *Test* was cancelled with one final hurrah that New Year as – you're ahead of me here – *87 Whistle Test 88*, where David Hepworth talked to Bruce Springsteen, John Peel introduced Zimbabwean music stars The Bhundu Boys, there was a showing of the irony-free documentary *U2 – Outside It's America* before a final 100- minute highlights retrospective of the series 16-year history. A fine ending to a very important part of British music TV. Just a shame about that live Gary Glitter concert from Bournemouth in the middle of it.

Back to **1985** and the start of a BBC One tradition that continues to this day – the big end-of-year chat show – and as he's already been doing admirably at 7pm three times a week it was fitting to book a special late-night shift for *Wogan*, a slot Terry would also fill with his ample Irish cheeks the following year. Over on Channel 4, meanwhile, they've allowed Billy Connolly to preside over the year's end with *At Last It's Hogmanay*, whilst **1986** featured the decidedly odd *Come Dancing with Jools Holland*, a spin off from C4's pop show "The Tube", which starts as a sitcom of sorts with the titular pianist being interrupted by Ruby Wax, Uri Geller, and Phil Pope, Julia Hills and Rory McGrath of the controversial "Who Dares Wins"[55]. Eventually, the special becomes a sort of proto-Hootenanny with the now standard mix of well-meaning but dull rhythm and blues jams in front of an invited audience which includes both the ghastly Leon Brittan and Derek Hatton. Despite resembling Jools' current Later... get-togethers there's none of the slickness from those shows here (a po-faced link about an attempt to talk to Winnie Mandela breaking down leaves him seemingly in a foul mood) and the wheels feel like they're about to fall off any second. The one member of the "Who Dares Wins" cast not present at all was Jimmy Mulville because he was hosting *The New Year Show* on ITV at the same time with Muriel Gray plus Lloyd Cole and *"new comedy discovery Craig Ferguson"*. Wonder what happened to him etc.

---

55 One notable moment features another "Who Dares Wins" cast member, the timid Tony Robinson, having to break through a fake wall because Rik Mayall and Ade Edmondson hadn't turned up as advertised.

Aside from Two's marathon Whistle Test finale, **1987** marks possibly the low point of New Year TV as midnight brings a confusingly scheduled new *EastEnders* on BBC One and Des O'Connor on ITV *"linking up"* with journalist and general pain in the arse Derek Jameson in Trafalgar Square, which makes that Gary Glitter gig on Two seem suddenly more inviting...

1988 is a considerable improvement, though, as BBC One begins its seven-year association with a much-respected Australian critic and comic. *Clive James on 88* began a relationship with the Corporation that would continue each 31st December until 1994 when Clive went back to ITV. Also in '88, there's an opportunity to look back at the great work for charity that so many celebrities didn't like to talk about with "Comic Relief's Nose at Ten" (BBC One) showing highlights from the first ever Red Nose telly special, and "Every Penny Counted – Telethon '88" on ITV remembering the third channel's 27-hour "me too" equivalent that may have been the dullest thing ever transmitted up to that point. ITV finally saw out the year with *Cilla's Goodbye '88* in which Cilla Black returned to New Year's Eve after two decades with the surprisingly decent support of Harry Enfield, Kenny Everett, Kim Wilde and Ned Sherrin. Although fans of garbage will be pleased to know that it did still find a slot for Jim Davidson. A sequel of sorts followed in **1989** with the bloated 210-minute *Cilla's Goodbye to the '80s* starring everyone from Sir John Mills to Barry McGuigan with Alexei Sayle, Hale and Pace and Jonathan Ross representing the new breed of stars whilst Cliff Richard, Denis Norden and Michael Aspel were on hand to remind folks they were still watching ITV so not to get too excited. Younger viewers might have been better off sticking with *Eighties –* BBC Two's three-hour *"rock review of the decade"* produced by the arts strand "The Late Show" and featuring clips from everything from "Top of the Pops" to "Crackerjack". Channel 4 finished out the year with the sort of programme that would've been could only truly have been made for only one network – the fantastically naughty, innuendo-stuffed Christmas pudding that was **Sticky New Year with Julian Clary,** a live version of recent hit pseudo game show "Sticky Moments" – a silly and hugely enjoyable game show conceived by Clary and one of the channel's future stars Paul Merton.

90s: New Men and Newman and Baddiel

Channel 4 continued the trend of giving their big new show the New Year's slot as **Vic Reeves New Year's Eve Big Night Out** in **1990** took to the airwaves. It was much the same as the series, but with rare real-world guests including Mark Wingett from ITV's long-running police serial "The Bill" interrogating Reeves over his dodgy businesses and Kim Wilde and Michael Starke – better known as Sinbad from "Brookside" – as *"pop stars subjected to trial by plum"* in a slanted competition. (*"It's Large!"*) Very little mention is given of New Year as the programme was pre-recorded and it was frustratingly left off the complete series DVD of "Vic Reeves' Big Night Out" released in 2005 – although it can now be found on the station's All4 on-demand service. **1991** offers little more exciting than the first UK TV showing of **Mad Max** on BBC Two followed by **This Is Spinal Tap** whilst most ITV regions just stuck on a second showing of the 1986 comedy **Down And Out In Beverly Hills**. Altogether more memorable for that channel was December 31st **1992** – the date which saw several much-loved ITV regional channels going off the air after losing their franchises in to a money-grabbing bidding war the previous year And so it was that Television South (TVS), Thames, Television

South West (TSW) and TV-am were replaced by Meridian, Carlton, Westcountry and GMTV. To those young enough not to remember when ITV was still known by its regional stations, well... just say a prayer for the sobbing middle-aged men in the "I LOVE IDEANTS" jumpers clinging desperately to a sticky autograph of Gus Honeybun. Elsewhere, Channel 4 once again knocked it out of the park with the 90-minute live spectacular *The Big Breakfast End Of Year Show* with a late but not especially naughty edition of its hugely successful new morning show.

As **1993** became the spanking new 1994, BBC2 greeted the New Year for the first time with *Jools Holland's Hootenanny* a slightly underwhelming bill featuring Sting, the Gipsy Kings and Sly and Robbie. The programme, originally spun off from "The Late Show" (hence the *Later* tag), would steadfastly stick to its midnight slot for several years, bar a brief trot to the 30th in 1999 for millennial reasons, before becoming the 11pm-ish slot behemoth in 2002, where it remains every year to this day.

And for our final programme of this exhausting look back at the New Years of old it's only right we return to Scotland for BBC One's *Hogmanay Live* returning to the more traditional ways of old. Gordon Kennedy off of "Absolutely" and the Tunes adverts, and Lorraine Kelly with music from Edwyn Collins, Eddi Reader and Gary Glitt... oh forget it...

January 1st

In order to convey the full majesty of New Years Day for this introduction I have drunk eight pints and eaten exactly the right amount of the very worst pepperoni available from "Almost Italian Steve's Supa Pizzer" at quarter to five in the early hours of a beautiful new year. Excuse me, I just have to do a thing...

Of course, not everyone spends New Year's Day feeling like they came out worse in a fight with an articulated Shrek. I have personally spent the last five 1). ill, 2). at a friend's house, 3). in bed, 4). ill, 5). classified by NATO (but probably ill.) The one thing that unquestionably links all of those experiences is that the TV was on somewhere in all of them. It's one of the few legitimate guilt-free days to snuggle under a blanket, finish off the Christmas chocs and watch television all day and night without the fear of a random auntie suddenly appearing from nowhere like an episode of "The Walking Dead" sponsored by M&S's Chocolate Macaroon Assortment.

Usually on January 1st the terrestrial channels offer up a big meaty drama, possibly the first episode of a running series, as if seeing some no doubt flawed protagonist try to get through a difficult scenario is an analogy for going back to work the following day, possibly still hungover. There's also the same 15 hours of soaps and daytime programming they can't be bothered to change as if terrorists have threatened to blow up Cheshire if they don't get their regularly scheduled episodes of "Homes What Are Being Sold" and "Some Antiques Shit"..

Yes, its January and bugger all has changed. So let's watch some TV and block out those voices telling us all the resolutions we're going to break. Resolution 1: ~~Don't read the following final chapter~~....oops. Sorry.

Wednesday, 1ˢᵗ January, 1958

2.45pm: Mainly for Women (BBC)

Having got their own hour on the wireless since 1946 now these 'women' were after their own TV slots too! This was a strange hodgepodge of smaller shows under a banner title including: "Your Own Time" – a "light-hearted magazine for younger women" (close your eyes throughout older women!), a puff piece for new historical drama "Dangerous Exile" with *"some of the costumes worn in the film"* and part 32 of "Quick and Easy Dressmaking" as Diana Crutchley demonstrates the "Jersey Hood" which it turns out is clothing and not something to do with "The Sopranos". "I'd Like to Know" sadly isn't a performance of the 1995 Supergrass' track but a report from Roma Fairley who *"finds out from Phyllis Allan and 'Smuggler' how to train a high-school horse"*. Representing the cherry on the cake (also: no cake for you, you've a dress to fit in, love) is a selection of "Tunes at the Piano" performed by Roy Wallis. And if any men were watching that, please turn yourself in at the nearest "Mainly for Women" Correction Centre.

Friday, 1ˢᵗ January, 1965

3.00pm: Film: The Gay Dog (ITV)

"A miner, Jim Gay, owns a greyhound, Raving Beauty, which has been very successful in races at the local stadium. But his bets on the dog are not winning him much money, so Gay hits upon a plan..."

Settle down. This is a 1954 British comedy film of course, none of the other, that's right out. It's a feast of British acting talent with the hugely popular Wilfred Pickles leading his Gay family (stop that) including Megs Jenkins and a 21 year old Petula Clark just starting her musical career. "Doctor Who" fans will delight in seeing early companion Ian (William Russell), "Meddling Monk" Peter Butterworth and even the Third Doctor 'imself Jon Pertwee in the key role of "Betting Man". How queer! (gay) (homosexual) (tray on head)

Thursday, 1ˢᵗ January, 1970

7.30pm: The Jugg Brothers (BBC One)

"Two brothers work as caretakers in a block of flats in London. They pass their time by competing for the perks of the job..."

A totally forgotten "Comedy Playhouse" pilot, starring Blakey and The One With The Teeth Who Wasn't Reg Varney off On The Buses but written by them as well. This was the first of the ninth run of comedy pilots that had earlier produced Steptoe and Son and The Liver Birds but none of the four shows went to series here. As well as The Juggs, there was Myles Rudge's "An Officer and a Gentleman", "Joint Account"[56], and "Who's Your Friend?" in which Bernard Cribbins plays *"a professional escort"*. Despite Lewis and Grant's failure here they would go on to write 12 episodes of "On the Buses" together as if that's something to be in any way proud of. Smashin' Juggs.

---

56 Not the 1989 Peter Egan/Hannah Gordon one. This has a horrible synopsis: *Keith Barron stars as Rodney, who had recently married Celia who is a dreadful cook.*

Saturday, 1ˢᵗ January, 1972

5.45pm: Disney Parade: No Smoking (BBC One)

"Goofy is determined to be hale, if not hearty, by not inhaling."

A troubling 1951 cartoon short featuring Goofy as a regular schmoe who loves nothing more than puffing down a tab but decides to quit because of the ill effects. His resolve is tested by all of his co-workers smoking away and the final half of the cartoon is his desperate search for a cig. It's played for laughs but seeing Goofy suffering from nicotine withdrawal and crawling on the floor fighting tramps for discarded stogies is just disturbing, even more than him smoking in the first place. Unsurprisingly this short didn't make many appearances on TV in the ensuing years although an edit was made to have Goofy saying he was quitting for good after being given an exploding cigar in the final scene. It's in especially dubious taste when you discover that Goofy's voice actor Pinto Colvig had lung disease at the time of recording and became a key advocate for fag packets displaying warnings before he died of lung cancer in 1967, just like Walt Disney himself the previous year.

Thursday, 1ˢᵗ January, 1976

9.30pm: Supermind (BBC One)

"In this fourth year of Mastermind. past winners have been invited to compete for the title Supermind."

When proper intelligence based quizzes didn't require Victoria Coren's busters as a public lure, this was a pitched battle between the winners of the first four "Mastermind" finals Nancy Wilkinson (who won this special), Patricia Owen, Elizabeth Horrocks and rather spoiling the matriarchal tone 1975's champ John Hart who answered questions on the diverse topics "Athens 500–400 BC", "Rome 100–1 BC" and "Athens 500–400 BC" again[57]. At the time of writing, three of BBC Two's "Eggheads" team are former Mastermind winners (Chris Hughes in 1983, Kevin Ashman in 1995, Pat Gibson in 2005), but only one of the Chasers on ITV's "The Chase" (Shaun Wallace in 2004) had previously tasted victory in the black chair. Richard Osman was not available for comment.

Saturday, 1st January, 1977

10.10am: Coronation Day 1953 (BBC Two)

"With unique archival material from one of the earliest tele-recordings ever made, we invite you to relive Coronation Day Celebrations"

Yes, its seven fabulous hours of soft-focus black and white fuzzy Royal footage as the perfect accompaniment to that hangover. Forget "Swap Shop" kids! No "Grandstand" for you Dad! This is what you want to be watching! An intriguing experiment for television in 1977 and one rarely copied nowadays, outside of BBC Parliament's occasional Election Night coverage repeats. For those watching on catch-up, the service began at 11:20 with Liz being crowned at half-twelve. I wonder if she tuned in for it? *"One thinks that crown makes my arse look huge...."*

---

57 Contestants were initially permitted to return to their first
    specialist subject if they made the grand final. This ended in 1992.

10.30pm: New Year with the Fosters (ITV)

"New Year's Eve in South London and the Foster family is dismayed to hear that an elderly neighbour is so poor, she may be going hungry. Charitably, they invite her to supper, and, alarmingly she brings with her a home-made meat loaf to share with them. What is it made with?"

With many British sitcom hits adapted for America in the seventies ("Man About the House" becoming "Three's Company", Steptoe becoming Sanford etc.), "The Fosters" reversed the trend being based on the hit US series "Good Times" (CBS, 1974–79). The American show had begun as a more serious minded comedy, handling big issues, but would soon devolve into a cheap catchphrase-led vehicle for breakout character JJ and his repetitive *"Dy-no-mite!"* phrase which took the country by storm. Over here in the UK, this LWT sitcom about a modern black family living in London was toned down a little with JJ became loveable layabout Sonny, played by an enthusiastic Lenny Henry (aged just 17 when the series began in April 1976). This episode, featuring guest star Irene Handl, was taken pretty much wholly from a second season "Good Times" episode titled "The Dinner Party" in which the family suspect an impoverished elderly neighbour has made a meatloaf from dog food[58]. The Foster family would return for a second and final series of 13 episodes in April 1977. When that ended, Lenny graduated to Saturday morning favourite "TISWAS" and general super-stardom whilst his on-screen parents Norman Beaton and Carmen Munroe would reunite, again as a married couple, in the even more successful sitcom "Desmond's" from 1989 to 1994 on Channel 4.

---

58 She hasn't.

Sunday, 1ˢᵗ January, 1978

11.00pm: John Wayne (BBC One)

"Frank Sinatra hosts an affectionate tribute to 'Duke' Wayne."

R.I.P. "Dukes-o". We shall miss 'im greatly, gone before his time and... what do you mean he wasn't dead? He actually carked on June 11ᵗʰ 1979, you say? Oh well, they'll get another showing out of this CBS special from November 1977 then! The sort of showbiz shindig that audiences used to lap up, this event was staged to celebrate 50 years in the movies for the walnut-faced cowsman although quite why some guests are there is a bit of a mystery; as Charles Bronson states in his introduction, *"I have never worked with John Wayne nor have I had the pleasure of meeting him until this evening..."* Next week: Chuck Norris on "The Krzysztof Kieślowski I Never Knew".

Thursday, 1ˢᵗ January, 1981

10.20pm: Wood and Walters – Two Creatures Great and Small (ITV)

"Victoria Wood – who also wrote the show – and Julie Walters have a funny turn in the studio, complete with song and dance."

Having already gone through the talent show mangle, sang topical songs for "That's Life" and written several successful plays, Victoria Wood finally got her first half hour with regular collaborator Julie Walters as moral support. This pilot was produced for Granada by Peter Eckersley but his tragic death before a full series could be made left Wood distraught and with no desire to continue. Eventually one series emerged, beginning exactly a year later on 1st January 1982. Despite the circumstances in which it was made there's a lot of strong material throughout and it's a signpost towards the amazing work that would follow when she moved to the BBC.

Saturday, 1st January, 1983

9.15am: Sesame Street's Big Bird in China (ITV)

"A special show, with music, for all the family. Sesame Street's Big Bird travels through China in search of the legendary Phoenix."

It had taken a while – nearly the whole of the 1970s in some areas of the UK – but by the early 1980s "Sesame Street" could be seen in most of the country after great controversy in its early days over worries of Americanising our youth and influencing children to paint themselves green and live in a bin or something. Considering that animosity it might be surprising to learn that this special actually premièred in this country five months ahead of the US, where it would later win the 1984 Emmy for Outstanding Children's Program[59]. Caroll Spinney, the man inside the bird until his 2018 retirement, had already visited China as part of a Bob Hope spectacular in 1979 and was inspired to return for this special. Its appeal does tend to hinge on whether you find Big Bird a lovable awkward babe or an annoying ignorant git but the opening song by the full cast is great (*"You'll meet some new people! / Get some new kicks! / See some new places! / You'll eat with sticks! / In Chiiiinnaaaa....."*) and it's good to see footage from an earlier time before the

---

59 Beating "Grandpa, Will You Run with Me?", "Skeezer" and "The Snow Queen – A Skating Ballet". No me neither.

country was modernised a little. The yellow peril would return to the Orient for 1989's "Big Bird in Japan". I just hope he doesn't discover them used knicker vending machines.

7.15pm: Jane (BBC Two)

"How far will Jane uncover herself in her efforts to keep England's defence plans under wraps? Find out in this wartime adventure story starring Glynis Barber as the famous strip-cartoon heroine."

A technically stunning piece of work at the time "Jane" used the latest in computer graphics to make actors seem as if they were in a living comic strip complete with thought bubbles and panels, befitting its newspaper roots as "Jane's Journal or the Diary of a Bright Young Thing" which ran from 1932 to 1959 in the Daily Mirror. The frequently half-dressed Jane Gay was brought to TV with scripts by Mervyn Haisman and music by Neil Innes as 10-minute instalments every night in early August 1982 with a 45-minute omnibus which was repeated here. Featuring an eclectic cast including duck walking comic Max Wall, Suzanne Danielle as a Nazi villain and dachshund Fritz The Dog "as himself". Jane and her cast of comic characters would return in September 1984 for a sequel entitled "Jane in the Desert". Screenwriter Haisman was hired off the back of this to script a big budget movie version of the character. 1987's "Jane and the Lost City" featured Kirsten Hughes in the title part and contained a rare big screen role for Jasper Carrott but it lacked the on-screen graphics that had made it so memorable on TV. Meanwhile, on the other side, for those who don't like comedy...

7.15pm: Get Knighted (Channel 4)

"An hour of antics by The Barron Knights."

Oh. The collected "antic" of Duke D'Mond and his bunch of pals has been an acquired taste since they first hit the UK charts in 1964 with their low-hanging-fruit reworded medleys of popular hits of the time. After an initial spurt of success a "barren" period followed and many thought they'd seen the back of the chart sound clowns. 1978's "Live in Trouble" single broke the wonderful silence with a smash No. 7 hit containing "hilarious" "send-ups" of "You Make Me Feel Like Dancing" (titled "My Tailor Took My Pants In") and "Float On" which adds just what the original was missing – comedy Irishmen and "pooves". Although their second wind in the charts didn't last much past 1979, this Channel 4 programme allowed them to make videos for several songs, both covers and originals, whilst performing others live in front of an audience. Further specials aired including "Twice Knightly" on Christmas Day 1983. Meanwhile the band are still touring today with one whole original member – Peter "Peanut" Langford.

11.15pm: Bennett Bites Back (ITV)

"Hungover, irritable, depressed? You will be..."

And here's more top flight comedy from Lennie Bennett who had briefly been part of a successful double act with Jerry Stevens on the BBC before both panicked and ran in opposite directions. This was Bennett's short lived topical chat show which I include mostly for its incongruous pairing in the ITV schedule with...

11.45pm: Saturday Night Live (ITV)

"Cry your eyes out with sentiment in tonight's less funny than usual show,. Paul and Art come together to sing live their greatest heart-throbbing hits. Plus other guest stars Randy Newman, The Muppets and the regular team."

Now into its 43rd season running into 2019, "Saturday Night Live" has received a bit of a raw deal when it comes to repeats in the UK, cropping up over the decades on BBC Two, MTV, Paramount, ITV2 and Sky One. But here it was ITV (in various regions) showing an edit of the second-ever episode from 1975. At that point the format wasn't properly in place and as such the classic original cast featuring John Belushi, Jane Curtin and Chevy Chase only appear for around 45 seconds, in between a whopping eight songs by Paul Simon, three in a much hyped reunion with Art Garfunkel.

As for The Muppets, it wasn't the felt friends we know but special all-new creations set in the more adult themed The Land of Gorch about the inhabitants of a strange alien world which ran in the first 10 editions before being scrapped. This kind of curiosity was normally snipped from non-live repeat editions but may have been kept here to capitalise on the continuing British love for all things cute and Henson-made. The late, quick-to-temper but brilliant SNL writer Michael O"Donoghue was happy to see the fuzzy buggers go, quoted by Bernie Brillstein in the terrific oral history of the series, "Live From New York: An Uncensored History of Saturday Night Live", O'Donoghue reputedly said: "I won"t write for felt."

Friday, 1st January, 1988

8.30am: Australia Live – Celebration of a Nation (Channel 4)

"A live programme from Australia watched all over the world, to celebrate the 200th anniversary of the country from Ayers Rock to Adelaide from the Sydney Opera House to the Barrier Reef."

A vivid memory of my childhood Christmases is a newly eight-year-old me being surprised that my parents didn't want to get up early and watch this live New Year's Day broadcast from Oz to mark the bicentenary of some British ships rocking up on the shore there. Naturally it had to include Paul Hogan, Clive James and Dame Edna Everage who were all at their peak. This was especially true of Hogan, who had made Australia fashionable pretty much overnight, thanks to "Crocodile Dundee" being second only to "Top Gun" as 1986's highest grossing film in the US. The film's director Peter Faiman was also behind the camera for this four-hour behemoth which also linked up to all over the country like a slightly warmer version of Noel up the Telecom Tower. What's all that about?

7.00pm: Wogan (BBC One)

"On the evening after the night before, there'll be red noses all round in the Wogan studio – as Terry invites Dawn French, Stephen Fry and Hugh Laurie, among others, to launch Comic Relief."

Another unique moment of history here as Terry Wogan welcomes a lot of still pretty obscure comedians to a mainstream sudience as they announce the launch of the first ever Red Nose Day and Comic Relief telethon just a month later on 5th February, 1988. Fry, Laurie, French and Wogan all drink red beer and show off the soon-to-be ubiquitous red noses. The audience seem unsure how to react, as if it's a top wheeze by the alternative comics (Dawn suggests she'll be *"pulling people's trousers down and laughing at their genitalia"* whilst Fry claims they're being sponsored every time they say *"haemorrhage"*). It all seems strange now, given Comic Relief is a permanent British institution but also rather exciting of what is still to come. Even musical guests The Stranglers are cajoled into wearing the red noses too whilst performing their generally unnecessary cover of "All Day and All of the Night". Stonking.

Monday, 1st January, 1990

10.30am: Interceptor (ITV)

"Annabel Croft tries to outwit the devilish Interceptor as she directs Sarah Hollis from Wrexham and Clive Harris from Herts, over land and sea."

Effectively a reverse version of Channel 4's "Treasure Hunt" the game show "Interceptor" was ITV's big new commission in 1989 and featured contestants wearing clunky backpacks and trying not to get "zapped" in the back by an over-acting man in a helicopter whilst Not Annabel Giles tries to help. Vividly memorable and strangely beloved to people of a certain age – myself included – "Interceptor" was nonetheless axed after its initial seven episodes hence the rather inglorious timeslot for this final instalment. Luckily for producers Chatsworth Television they had a new game format coming up six weeks later on Channel Four entitled "The Crystal Maze"...

8.00pm: Mr Bean (ITV)

"A comedy special for New Year. Mr Bean, without many words, takes an exam, sunbathes and goes to church. He also drives badly."

In retrospect it seems quite unusual that the key members of the "Blackadder" team decided to follow up their already-classic vicious historical comedy with a mostly silent sketch show for prime-time ITV. Even with Rowan doing a very similar character in his live shows "Mr Bean" still seemed like a bit of a risk for writers Richard Curtis and, on this episode only, Ben Elton, as Atkinson's vocal delivery had been such a huge part of why his previous sitcom was great. It works brilliantly though and thus, for a few years, it became a genuinely special treat when a new Bean special was advertised in the schedules. It ran out of steam after the first few years and the latter shows aren't a patch on the earlier half- hours but Atkinson remains a joy to watch throughout..

8.30pm: The A–Z of TV (Channel 4)

"Tonight Channel 4 brings to your screens a three-hour extravaganza of nostalgia and TV history in celebration of productions which have been shown on British television over the years."

Tuesday 1st January, 1991

8.00pm: 1001 Nights of TV (Channel 4)

"Three hours of bizarre, powerful, off-the-wall and unashamedly nostalgic extracts plundered from the archives of British television with Michael Palin clocking up the scores."

And it only seems fitting that the last programmes I write about are themselves love letters to television not to mention hugely influential on my own interest in the magic lantern. Here Channel 4 dispensed with their earlier theme night practice of actually repeating full episodes, and instead ran lots of mini-features on the history of TV and its programmes starting on New Years Day 1990 with "The A–Z of TV" which took in everything from the start of the BBC in A is for Ally Pally right up to Zebedee...Time for bed.

Exactly a year later, "1001 Nights of TV" took "night" itself as its loose theme, with its most interesting segments including Wiped Nights (Alan Bennett highlighting how much is missing from the archives, including his own series), Dog Day Nights (Dogs on TV introduced by ace poet, comic and dog enthusiast John Hegley), Night School (an incredibly rare chance to see clips of early schools broadcasts), A Little Night's Music (Vic Reeves and Andy Kershaw selecting rare musical clips) and finally 2001 Nights which consists of *prognostications from the past about the future of television.*" I hope to Christ they didn't predict Love Island...

Closedown

In the early years of potentially being able to 'acquire' music I didn't own from the likes of Napster I would often hammer in random band names to try and increase my digital record collection. These were the wild west days of piracy and so a mixed bag would show up in the results, with two thirds almost certainly being Belgian bum videos. One friend who loves his Christmas music did the same and was amazed to find the following listed...

"so this is crismus – BEETLES.mp3"

Moving past the myriad of wrongness in there from artist to title and basic spelling and comprehension, this has always existed in my mind as a perfect example of how the specifics of nostalgia only really matter to a handful of enthusiasts and researchers like myself and how most people don't care what section of "Christmas Night with the Stars" still exist or what edits were made to the eighth repeat showing of "Alan at Large" because that's ultimately not what's important. What matters are the memories the TV in the corner gave us, both with the family and when we're alone, as a perennial key part of the British Christmas experience. And I hope this book has solved a few of those long-running arguments (and maybe added some new ones to boot!) and reminded you of some of those Decembers gone by. I hope it's brought a few laughs, maybe a few tears and a lot of bafflement at what the small screen used to get away with. Plus now you can experience the sharp hit of the festive period all year round without having to do anything as daft as actually inviting your family round!

No matter what time of the year it is: a very Merry Christmas and a Happy New Year. Even to you, Skeletor.

Acknowledgements

A big thank you to everyone who bought this book and made it a possibility in the first place along with any of my previous books. The biggest thanks go to Justin Lewis for his patient proofing, Tim Worthington for his constant encouragement and Bob Stanley who created the amazing front cover.

Thanks also to inspirations, general rocks of friendship and all round 'meaningless-to-anyone-else' goodness... Emma Pears, Tim Worthington, Phil Catterall, Michael Spencer, Louise Nilon, James Wallace, Shona Brunskill, Ryan Davies, Keeley Collington, Ali & Robin, Russell Hillman, Justin Lewis, Faye & James Beedle, Patch Kelly, Josh Tildesley, Sarah Hammond, Damian Curran, Luke & Sal, Garreth Hirons, Jenna Maleckyj, Joe Tilston, Kayley Cookson, Chris Eastwood, Rich Nelson, John Rivers, Mickey Waddington, Joe Dinsdale, Bonita Wood, Michael Watmough, Sean Howe, Katie Armitage, Iain Hepburn, Matt Lee, Chris & Kylie Bate, Darrell Maclaine-Jones, Luke and Lid, Louis Barfe, Jonny Mohun, Jonathan Sloman, Simon Scott, Ian Greaves, Andy Hardaker, Adam Smith, Chris Lyons, The Jenningses, David Balston and Jonny Mohun.

It is dedicated to the memory of Shirley Blackburn who was a martyr to her telly schedule and hugely missed.

We now conclude our broadcast day. Please remember to turn off your book.

sine wave

Other Books By This Author

"Kill Your Television"

A love letter to all things televisual - taking in everything from ALF to Z Cars and paying tribute to the programmes, presenters, sounds and strange spin-offs that made the flashing square box in the corner of the room great.

"Talk About The Passion: New Adventures In Old Pop Culture"

A best of my old pop culture fanzine "TATP" plus over thirty pages of new material from myself and Tim Worthington.

"Your Starter For Ben"
"Never Mind The Quizbooks"
"Remotely Interesting"
"The Long Quiz Goodnight"

This is my range of quirky trivia quiz books and cover general knowledge, music and TV respectively.

All available at:

www.benbakerbooks.co.uk

or search Amazon for "Ben Baker" for Kindle

Printed in Great Britain
by Amazon

49069864R00119